HEART
OF A HUSKY

Determination, Perseverance, and a Quest for a National Championship

MEL THOMAS

CO-CAPTAIN OF THE 2007-2008 UCONN WOMEN'S BASKETBALL TEAM

keen custom media

TO ORDER THIS BOOK, PLEASE GO TO:
MELTHOMAS.COM

OPYRIGHT

2009 BY MEL THOMAS
PUBLISHED BY KEEN CUSTOM MEDIA
1700 MADISON ROAD
CINCINNATI, OH 45206
WWW.KEENCUSTOMMEDIA.COM

LIBRARY OF CONGRESS CATALOGING-IN-PUBLICATION DATA

THOMAS, MEL.
HEART OF A HUSKY : DETERMINATION, PERSEVERANCE, AND A QUEST FOR A NATIONAL CHAMPIONSHIP /
BY MEL THOMAS.
  P. CM.
   ISBN-13: 978-0-9647083-3-4
   ISBN-10: 0-9647083-3-7
1. UNIVERSITY OF CONNECTICUT--BASKETBALL. 2. CONNECTICUT HUSKIES (BASKETBALL TEAM)
3. BASKETBALL FOR WOMEN--CONNECTICUT. 4. WOMEN BASKETBALL PLAYERS--CONNECTICUT. I. TITLE.
GV885.43.U44T56 2009
796.323'630974643--DC22
   2008048913

FRONT COVER PHOTO COURTESY OF **THE HARTFORD COURANT / STEPHEN DUNN**
BACK COVER PHOTO COURTESY OF **AP / KIICHIRO SATO**

EDITED BY
Warren Witherell

COVER AND INTERIOR DESIGNED BY
Stephen Sullivan

DEDICATION

To the Cincinnati Children's Hospital medical staff

When I was three years old, I became very sick. Typically, I was always full of
energy, but suddenly I was noticeably lethargic and wouldn't move from the
couch. My parents took me to the hospital, where I was initially diagnosed
with dehydration. I was released after receiving an IV, which was expected to
perk me up. After showing no signs of improvement, my mother's intuition
told her something was seriously wrong. She called our family doctor,
pleading for his immediate help. He trusted her instincts and agreed to meet
her at the hospital on his day off. She refused to leave until they admitted me
for further testing.

It turned out I had Hemolytic-Uremic Syndrome (HUS), which shredded
my red blood cells and damaged my kidneys' filtering cells—eventually
shutting down my kidneys. I was in the hospital on peritoneal dialysis for a
month, until finally, by the grace of God, my kidneys began to function again.
From that moment on, I was one of the happiest children in the world.

If it were not for the medical care I received, I wouldn't be here today.
I am incredibly thankful for the amazing people at Children's Hospital who
gave me the gift of life.

About the Author

When she was in sixth grade, Mel Thomas fell in love with the sport of basketball. It became the central focus of her life. But basketball was more than just a game for Mel. It was the crucible in which her character and values were formed. It was a world where she found the friends and mentors who have been most instrumental in her development as a person.

Mel Thomas is a native of Cincinnati, Ohio. During her senior season at Mount Notre Dame High School, she led her team to a perfect 28-0 record and the school's first Division I Ohio State Basketball Championship.

Mel joined the UConn Huskies in 2004, where she continued the tradition of UConn women's basketball student-athletes who have succeeded at the highest levels both academically and athletically. Mel was a three-time Big East Academic All-Star, and is a graduate of UConn's highly-regarded School of Business.

Mel was named co-captain of her team in both her junior and senior seasons. In her senior year, she played a key role in UConn's winning the Big East regular season and tournament championships, and in their run to the NCAA Final Four. Mel finished her career with 1,098 points and ranked fourth in UConn history in three-pointers made with 224.

Mel was a member of the United States Pan American Games team in the summer of 2007 as the U.S. won the gold medal for the first time since 1987.

If you talk to the coaches Mel has played for from sixth grade through college, you learn quickly that they love, respect, and admire her with all their hearts. When you finish this book, you will feel the same way about her.

TABLE OF
CONTENTS

FOREWORD *by Geno Auriemma*

MEL THOMAS will always be remembered as one of the toughest kids ever to play at UConn.

This is saying a lot, considering the many great players who have played here!

Mel became a great three-point shooter, but more importantly, she became invaluable to our program because of her grit and determination. She led our team in minutes played for a reason—I trusted her. I knew we were a better team with Mel on the court.

I'm not surprised that Mel has been able to put into words what she embodies as a person. She is a tremendous inspiration to anyone who aspires to compete at the highest levels, in any endeavor.

The final game of our season during Mel's senior year, we lost in the Final Four. There is no doubt in my mind that if Mel were healthy and able to play, we would have won the game. Why? Because Mel Thomas is a winner—and a great role model for kids and adults of all ages.

PREFACE

For as far back as I can remember, my greatest dream was to win a National Championship. In my senior year, with the UConn basketball team, I was confident this would happen. I kept a journal of my daily life because I wanted to remember every minute of it.

The book you hold in your hands has been drawn from this journal.

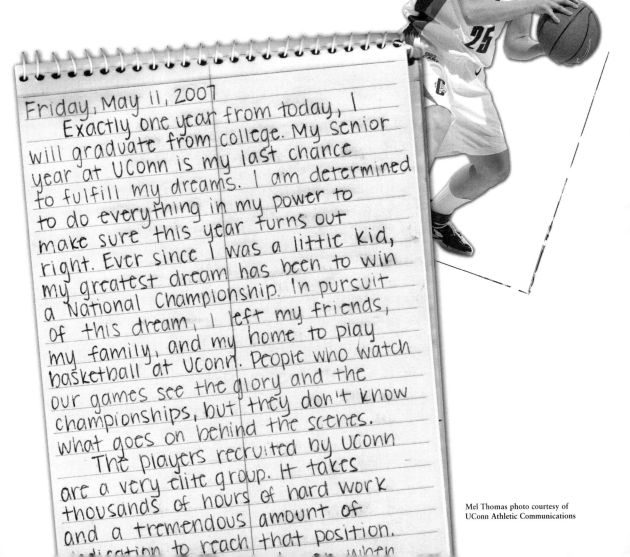

Friday, May 11, 2007

Exactly one year from today, I will graduate from college. My senior year at UConn is my last chance to fulfill my dreams. I am determined to do everything in my power to make sure this year turns out right. Ever since I was a little kid, my greatest dream has been to win a National Championship. In pursuit of this dream, I left my friends, my family, and my home to play basketball at UConn. People who watch our games see the glory and the championships, but they don't know what goes on behind the scenes.

The players recruited by UConn are a very elite group. It takes thousands of hours of hard work and a tremendous amount of dedication to reach that position.

Cast of Characters

My teammates and coaches have been the most influential people in my life at UConn. Here's the cast of characters who made up our team for the 2007-2008 school year.

Seniors

#11 KETIA SWANIER / "KEESH"

Ketia is a Georgia peach and a 5'7" point guard. She's a great passer whose hard work and unselfish play energize our team. Ketia is unbelievably fast with the ball so whenever she is on the court, we can play a very up-tempo game. Ketia won the 2008 Sixth Man Award for the Big East Conference. She grew up in a military family. Both of her parents served in the United States Army and retired as E8 Sergeants. They instilled strong values in their daughter and taught her to be disciplined both on and off the court.

24 CHARDE HOUSTON / "CHAR CHAR"

Charde is a 6'1" forward from San Diego. She's been blessed with an incredible amount of natural ability. Charde holds the California high school scoring record of 3,837 points. She is completely unpredictable. She may glide into a room on roller skates or jump into a handstand at totally unexpected times! Charde loves to dance and she's incredibly good at it. She gave me dance lessons our freshmen year in hopes that someday I'd reach her level. I don't see it happening any time soon.

#44 BRITTANY HUNTER / "BRIT"

Brit is a 6'3" center from the great state of Ohio. She is a terrific rebounder who plays with intense passion. She is one of the very best centers in the country, but her playing time has been limited by a chronic knee injury. If she could play normal minutes, Brit would be a true superstar. She is extremely extroverted. Brit is loud and funny and always keeps our team entertained. She can sit in an empty room with anyone and find some way to make it fun.

Juniors

#20 RENEE MONTGOMERY / "NE NE"

Renee is a 5'7" point guard from West Virginia. She is a co-captain, and a terrific leader of our team. Renee is a great shooter and ball handler, and is very athletic. Renee is a small player, but she has a huge presence on the court. Through sheer willpower, she can inspire her team and take over a game at any time. Renee believes she can do anything and convinces others they can too. She is incredibly competitive. When I play one-on-one games with her, she talks so much junk that sometimes I just want to slap her. Renee loves musicals more than anything and is always singing show tunes around her apartment.

#32 KALANA GREENE / "LA LA"

Kalana is a 5'10" guard from Charleston, South Carolina. She is incredibly athletic, and is a great rebounder and slasher. Kalana is difficult to guard because she has a quick first step and runs the court really well. She is also one of UConn's best defensive players. Kalana is often asked to shut down the other team's top scorer. Kalana excels in the classroom and runs a successful DJ business.

#2 TAHIRAH WILLIAMS / "T"

T is a 6'0" guard/forward from Montclair, New Jersey. When she's on the floor, she plays extremely hard and brings speed and energy to the game. When T made her official recruiting visit to UConn, everyone thought she was crazy because she was entirely too excited the whole time. We could have sat her in a chair in front of a blank wall and she would have been happy. She says more ridiculous, off-the-wall things than anyone else on our team. She's always good for a laugh, and she makes the world a brighter place. T genuinely cares for people, and will do anything for anyone in a heartbeat.

#51 CASSIE KERNS / "CASSALA"

Cassie is a 6'3" post player from Valparaiso, Indiana. She is a smart basketball player who does all the little things right. My first memory of Cass was seeing her in the stands when we played at Notre Dame. She was wearing a metallic dress with matching boots and an excessive amount of jewelry. I remember thinking, "Well, that's different." And that's exactly what Cassie is—different. She's an incredible artist and that contributes to her unique sense of style and perception of the world.

Sophomores

#31 TINA CHARLES / "BINA"

Tina is a 6'3" center from New York City, and she makes sure everyone knows it. Tina was the 2006 National High School Player of the Year. In 2007, her first season at UConn, she won the Big East Conference Freshman of the Year award. Tina is very athletic and has great mobility in the post. She can be a monster on defense. Tina is a very kind person who has a completely goofy, fun-loving side. She is truly a little kid at heart. She loves to watch cartoons, and she wears a different pair of cartoon character shorts every day.

#41 KAILI MCLAREN / "KAI"

Kaili is a 6'2" forward from Washington, D.C. She is the strongest player on our team and has a great outside shooting touch. Kaili loves basketball and spends a lot of time in the gym. On her recruiting visit, Kaili chased me with an umbrella, attempting to beat me up. From that moment, it was clear she was going to bring a lot of fun to our UConn family. Kaili has an incredibly outgoing personality, and everyone loves her. She has so many friends on campus that she can't walk anywhere without stopping to talk to at least 10 people.

#22 MEGHAN GARDLER / "MEGS"

Megs is a 6'0" guard from Philly. Whenever she enters a game, she has an immediate impact. She is an intelligent player who hustles all over the court. She disrupts offenses by getting in the passing lanes and is a good rebounder. Megs seemed very reserved on her official visit to UConn, but we soon realized that couldn't be further from the truth. Megs provides laughs for her teammates every day. To be as smart as she is, Megs says some pretty silly things, but she's a blond, what can we expect? She is an avid reader who always has a book in her hand. Megs knows the most random information that is completely useless.

#13 JACQUIE FERNANDES / "JAC" OR "CHAQUETA"

Jacquie is a Connecticut native and a 5'9" guard. She constantly looks out for her team's best interests. Jac does a lot of dirty work in both practice and games; and she always pushes her teammates to get better. She often stays after practice to rebound for others. Jacquie has a sarcastic sense of humor and can always be counted on to put in her two cents and make a smart comment.

Meghan

Tina

Kaili

Jacquie

Freshman

#30 LORIN DIXON / "LITTLE ONE"

Lorin is a 5'4" point guard from New York. She is incredibly fast and is always willing to learn. At practice, she studies the veteran point guards. She watches Ketia and Renee like a hawk, and mimics their every move. She's so short she could blend into an AAU tournament for fifth graders. Lorin always has a huge smile on her face, and it's contagious. Whenever she's in the locker room, the Disney Channel is on TV. For me, Lorin is the little sister I never had.

#23 MAYA MOORE / "MYRA"

Maya is a 6'0" guard from Georgia. She is only the second player in history to win the Naismith National High School Player of the Year award in both her junior and senior seasons. Though just a freshman, Maya is one of the best all-around players in the country. She is the first freshman to ever win the Big East Player of the Year award; and she was also honored as a First Team All-American.

Maya is an amazing athlete. She carries herself with extraordinary confidence, and is incredibly mature for her age. Most important, Maya is a sweetheart, and a genuinely nice person. She aspires to be the best in everything she does. She puts as much effort into her spiritual, academic, and family life as she does into her basketball. Maya embodies everything that could be good in a human being.

Photo courtesy of UConn Athletic Communications

Coaches

GENO AURIEMMA, HEAD COACH / "COACH"

Coach Auriemma was born in Italy in 1954. He immigrated to America when he was seven years old, and grew up in blue-collar towns around Philadelphia. He played high school ball in the Philly area, and started his coaching career there as well. When he took over the women's basketball program at UConn in 1985, the team had only experienced one winning season in the previous decade. Ten years later, the Huskies won their first National Championship. Coach Auriemma's teams added four more in 2000, 2002, 2003 and 2004.

Today, UConn Women's Basketball is recognized as one of the premier athletic programs in NCAA history. In 2006, Coach Auriemma was inducted in the National Basketball Hall of Fame.

Coach Auriemma's Philadelphia roots are deeply ingrained in his character and personality. He has a wise-guy sense of humor and a confident swagger. He runs a values-oriented program that demands hard work and a commitment to excellence in every part of his players' lives. Coach Auriemma constantly stresses the values of family, and inspires his team to play for one another.

CHRISTINE DALY, ASSOCIATE HEAD COACH / "CD"

CD was a star center at Rutgers University. She and Coach came to UConn together in 1985—the same year I was born. CD is one of the most personable, caring people in the world. She plays a large role in attracting recruits to UConn because she makes friends so easily, and so quickly earns their trust. CD works primarily with the post players at UConn, but she also demands perfection from every player in every drill at every practice. When it's time for work, CD is all business. She is also a strong enforcer of the high standards in personal conduct that our team is known for. CD puts her whole heart and soul into our program every day.

Photos courtesy of UConn Athletic Communications

CAST OF CHARACTERS

TONYA CARDOZA, ASSISTANT COACH / "TON"

Tonya played for the University of Virginia and is in her fourteenth season at UConn. She works primarily with the guards. She must be incredibly proud of all the First Team All-American guards she has coached at UConn. Tonya is always cool and laid back. Whenever players have concerns or frustrations, she is always willing to help.

JAMELLE ELLIOT, ASSISTANT COACH / "DOUBLE J"

Jamelle played at UConn and was a member of our 1995 National Championship team. She is in her eleventh season coaching the Huskies. Jamelle has legendary status at UConn as one of the "toughest" players ever to wear a Connecticut jersey. She was undersized in the paint but still one of the best rebounders in school history. She muscled her way to success on both ends of the court. I admire Jamelle's passion for the game. She coaches with as much heart and energy as she played.

JACK EISENMANN, DIRECTOR OF BASKETBALL OPERATIONS / "JACK"

Jack is in his seventh season with the program. He operates mostly "below the radar" but plays a big role in keeping many parts of our program running smoothly. Most important for our players, Jack is the man who maintains our film library. He's always happy to cut game tapes for players who want to study our opponents' offensive or defensive sets.

Photos courtesy of UConn Athletic Communications

CHAPTER 1
My First Love

FRIDAY, MAY 11, 2007

Exactly one year from today, I will graduate from college. My senior year at UConn is my last chance to fulfill my dreams. I am determined to do everything in my power to make sure this year turns out right. Ever since I was a little kid, my greatest dream has been to win a National Championship. In pursuit of this dream, I left my friends, my family, and my home to play basketball at UConn. People who watch our games see the glory and the championships, but they don't know what goes on behind the scenes.

The players recruited by UConn are a very elite group. It takes thousands of hours of hard work and a tremendous amount of dedication to reach that position. My basketball career began when I was in second grade. Two years later, I started playing year-round. I joined a traveling summer AAU team like so many other kids in America. By the time I was 12 years old, my parents knew I was going to be different. I played more sports than any other person I knew: volleyball, softball, soccer, track and field, diving, and dance. But as I got older, I slowly began to quit one after the other until I was playing only basketball and volleyball. In seventh grade, I refused to miss a basketball practice for a championship volleyball game. Needless to say, that was my last experience with volleyball.

Nothing else compared to basketball for me. I fell in love with the energy of the game. I was constantly running, jumping, and diving on the floor. In sixth grade, I began to seriously pursue the sport. Not a day passed when I didn't pick up a ball. I shoveled snow in my backyard, just so I could shoot. I wore football gloves to protect my hands from the cold. My family finally joined the YMCA so my fingers wouldn't fall off from frostbite. Every day after school, my mom picked me up and dropped me off at the Y. For hours, I shot hundreds and hundreds of jump shots, usually by myself. Once when I was sick with the flu, my mom asked me if I wanted to take a day off, but I refused. Other parents told my mom and dad I would get burned out on basketball. They didn't understand that the only person pushing me was me; and all the hours of practice and shooting were completely my choice. It was what I loved to do and what made me happy. The gym was a place where I could clear my mind and felt at home. The best times were when it was completely empty, and it was just me and my dreams. My parents never pushed me; they simply supported everything I did.

My dreams of a National Championship started early

I loved every second of it, but eventually basketball became an obsession. If I went one day without working out, I'd feel like I was letting myself down. I knew there were other players out there working hard and improving. So the easiest solution was to never take a day off, ever. There were years when I worked out literally every day of the year. Since no gyms were open on Christmas Day, I went out in my backyard and shot baskets, wearing my football gloves. I wouldn't leave for a vacation in Hawaii without my ball. There were no hoops there, so I just dribbled along the beach. Each night, I cuddled with my ball when I went to bed. It probably wasn't completely healthy. Everyone needs a day off once in a while, but nothing anyone said could convince me of that back then.

In school, my obsession with basketball did get me teased a little. When I was in seventh grade, I started at a new school. It was Catholic, so I was required to wear a uniform consisting of a skirt and a polo shirt. My first day of school, I played a pick-up game of basketball at recess. A girl named Ali Rohlfs, who later became my best friend and high school teammate, attended the same school. She told me years later, "My first memory of you was watching you play basketball with the boys at recess. All of a sudden, in your skirt, you dove on the blacktop for a loose ball. I was thinking 'what is wrong with this girl?' We all thought you were a weirdo!"

Some of my classmates threw boy/girl parties, which was a big deal for seventh grade. I remember one in particular, where everyone was inside dancing, playing spin the bottle, or trying to find a new boyfriend or girlfriend, but not me. I stayed outside shooting baskets the entire party. My other classmates came and went, playing basketball for a few minutes, but I never left the court. We were playing a game of three-on-three when the smallest, skinniest, least athletic girl in the entire class elbowed me in the nose. Blood began gushing down my face, so I ran inside to clean up. My only appearance inside the party was completely drenched in sweat and blood. I wasn't normal by any stretch of the imagination. I certainly didn't fit people's perceptions of a preteen girl. But I didn't want to be like everyone else. I desired to be something different. I was comfortable in my own skin and didn't feel the need to impress anyone. I refused to change who I was to fit in. Eventually, people accepted me for who I was.

When I was 13, I was the only girl in an all-boys league. The boys on my team *always* made fun of me for being a girl. Although it was all in good fun, it got old pretty quickly. I was resented by the boys on opposing teams. At one game, when I had a great first half against a really good team, their coach lost it in front of everyone. He yelled and screamed, "You're getting outrebounded, outhustled, and outplayed by a *girl*!" I didn't think about being a girl when I stepped on the court. I was a basketball player and didn't care what anyone thought.

I played for a local AAU team called Classicway until eighth grade. My early years of AAU were a great experience and taught me the fundamentals of the game. Everything was incredibly structured. For example, in order to teach us discipline, we had to memorize quotes by famous players and coaches like Vince Lombardi. Our team was a bunch of scrappy girls that won a lot more games than we should have based on talent alone. We won because we played with heart. We played together and hustled all over the floor. My coaches, Brad Lockhart and Derek Doerger, taught me to play hard and helped me develop my love for the game.

When I was playing for Coach Lockhart, a ball bounced off the bottom of the rim and hit my thumb during warm-ups. I didn't think much of it, but it was sore the whole game. During a time-out, I was holding it with my other hand to ease the pain. Coach Lockhart screamed at me, "Are you going to be a big baby and worry about your thumb the whole game or are you going to go out there and play?"

My Classicway AAU team

I looked up at him through my 11-year-old eyes and said, "I'm gonna play. I'm fine."

The next day I walked into practice with a bright blue cast halfway up my arm. I think he felt a little bad, but he still didn't give me much sympathy. My coaches taught me to be pretty tough from a young age.

A few years later, I had a fast break in a game and an opposing player fouled me hard—tackling me to the ground. My face slammed into the hardwood. I looked down at the floor and saw half a tooth lying on the ground. I picked it up, placed it on the scorer's table, and immediately walked back to the free throw line.

I became a better basketball player with each passing year, until stopping me was often the focal point of opposing teams. When teams played dirty and fouled me on purpose, I laughed it off because they couldn't do anything to me that I hadn't already done to myself. My grueling hours and hours of training prepared me for anything they threw at me. If they knocked me down, I got up smiling. They could bruise my body, but they couldn't touch my heart.

My freshman year of high school, I joined a different AAU program called All-Ohio Black. This team traveled to all the big Nike tournaments and got more exposure. I wanted to play in college, and All-Ohio Black was the best place to be noticed by a top-level program. I was far from the best athlete on our team, but I was the best shooter. I first heard about All-Ohio Black from one of their players, Barbara Turner. Our high school teams played each other, and after one of our games, she told me to come out for the team. Later, when Barbara went to UConn, I started to watch her games and developed my interest in the University of Connecticut.

The All-Ohio Black team was based in Columbus, which is an hour and a half from my house. During the spring and summer, I spent every weekend away from home. If we weren't playing in a tournament, we were practicing. We only practiced on weekends because everyone traveled too far to meet during the week. Our coach, JB, adopted us as his daughters for those months. Each weekend, about 10 of us would crowd into his basement to sleep. Needless to say, we were pretty close.

JB was very intense when he needed to be and had no problem cursing players out when they deserved it. However, we blew most teams out by 40 points, so he didn't have to be too serious. JB is a clown, which made playing for him a lot of fun. He would approach a player on the bench, tap her leg, and point to the scorer's table like he was putting her in the game. "Go get…" as if he was about to say a player's name, "…me a glass of water." The player would be excited about going into the game, and then he'd laugh hysterically as her face dropped when she caught onto the joke.

It seemed like we stayed at every Motel 6 in the country while traveling to all of our tournaments. With four of us to a room all the time, our duffle bags barely fit between the beds and the walls. We were always late to everything, even our games. Sometimes we'd show up at the gym, throw on our shoes, and run out for the opening tip without even taking a warm-up shot.

The Classicway and All-Ohio Black programs were completely different, but their main concept was the same. On both teams, basketball and fun went hand in hand. We worked hard, we played hard, we won, and winning was fun. It was that simple.

My All-Ohio Black AAU team

CHAPTER 2
Big Decisions

SATURDAY, MAY 12, 2009

The spring of my freshman year, my All-Ohio Black team lost a game in our first tournament. After that, we didn't lose again the rest of the summer. We were basically unstoppable, and every player on the team had Division I offers. It was then that the college recruiting process became more intense. Letters from different schools filled my mailbox every day. These letters introduced colleges to players they were interested in. The colleges were only allowed to send a recruit one form letter before September 1 of her junior year. The form letter asked general information such as the recruit's name, address, and hobbies. My freshman and sophomore years were consumed with filling out letter after letter that asked about my favorite food, television show, or book. At this point, I had received a letter from almost every Division I program in America.

After September 1 of the junior year, schools were free to send recruits an unlimited amount of mail. Most of the mail I received provided standard information about the school, newspaper articles on the team, and notes from the coaches. A few schools sent very unique letters. One sent me a sheet of paper with baking instructions on it. They said to put the paper in the oven at 350 degrees for 30 seconds until a message appeared. I crossed that school off my list right away! I received hundreds and hundreds of letters, but only consistently opened those from about 10 schools. I wasn't really interested in the whole process, but my mom was into it enough for both of us. She began by putting all the letters in photo albums. When those quickly filled up, she moved to boxes, organizing them alphabetically by school. She could recite all the coaches' names, the enrollment numbers, and the mascots. She knew everything.

One school sent me a long, three-page letter written in cursive. My mom came in my room and said, "Look how nice this is! It's handwritten by the head coach." I glanced at it but didn't look closely until there were three of them piled on my desk. When I finally looked at one, I knew it wasn't really handwritten. I found my mom and said, "Mom, it's not handwritten! It's just printed in cursive on the computer!" I thought it was hilarious, but my mom was angry because she thought the school was trying to trick us. So she changed her mind about that school pretty quickly!

After the letters, the next important date in the recruiting process came when coaches were allowed to contact recruits by phone. My first phone call came at 6:30 in the morning. I was constantly on the phone until 5:00 that night when my mom finally let me leave the house. I talked to a hundred people about exactly the same thing for almost 11 hours straight. My mom didn't let me tell anyone "no" on the first day because she thought everyone should have a chance. There were many schools I had never heard of and had no interest in; but that first day I talked to every coach who called. By lunchtime, the conversations started to flow together until it was impossible to remember who went with each school and what I said to which person.

Eventually, as I narrowed down my options, my relationships with the coaches became more personal. I met many wonderful people throughout this experience. The coaches were always considerate, and they spent their time talking with me every week. It was extremely difficult when I finally had to tell them I wasn't interested.

The phone calls helped me limit my choices to five schools. Home visits were the next step in the process. During these visits, coaches came to meet my family and have a home-cooked meal. There was no limit to the amount of home visits a recruit and her family could host. Cincinnati, Duke, Temple, Ohio State, and UConn visited my home. My mom cooked all kinds of foods that were representative of Cincinnati, so each coach could experience my hometown. She served Cincinnati's finest—Skyline chili, Montgomery Inn ribs, and Graeter's ice cream.

Each coach did something different to gain my interest. Duke's coaches brought a jersey and a diploma with my name on it. The coach of Cincinnati

My dad and I smiling for the Duke coaches

Playing host for the Cincinnati coaches

rang our doorbell, wearing the head of the bearcat mascot. Temple made a really nice photo-album presentation, and they were very down to earth. Coach Geno Auriemma from UConn just came, propped his feet up on the table, and drank all our wine.

Coach Auriemma was different from other coaches because he didn't kiss my butt or promise me anything. Some schools told me I would start, average a certain amount of points, or be the star of their program. None of those things were important to me; I just wanted to win. I wanted to play for the best program and was confident I would work hard enough to contribute to their success. I've been a winner my entire life, and I wanted that to continue. Coach told me, "This is what we do here. We work harder than every other team in the country, and that's why we win. If you want to be a part of that, then come. If you don't, then don't come." I spent much more time talking with other schools than with Connecticut, but it didn't matter. All the talking in the world could never make a school something it's not.

After the home visits, official visits to each college campus came next. Prospects could take five official visits that could last up to 48 hours. The schools paid for transportation to and from their campus, accommodation, meals, and entertainment. Recruits toured the facilities, met the players and coaches, and learned what their life would be like for the next four years. I went on four visits: Cincinnati, Ohio State, UConn, and Duke. The coach at Temple University, renowned player Dawn Staley, wanted me to visit as well, but I declined her offer. Although I liked her coaching style, her team was not one of the best in the country.

My first two visits were in Ohio at the University of Cincinnati and Ohio State. My mom wanted me to stay close to home, and the Cincinnati campus is only 15 minutes from our house. Both my parents are alumni and my brother is currently enrolled in U.C.'s law school. Our entire basement is decorated in Cincinnati's red and black, so home visits were a little awkward for all but the Cincinnati coaches.

My family has season tickets to the Bearcats football and basketball games. My uncle Roger and my father have attended every home game since I can remember. They have a unique story. Roger has Retinitis Pigmentosa, which caused him to go completely blind in his early twenties. He still goes to every game, alongside his Seeing Eye dog—Danny. My dad gives him play-by-play for each game, so he can "see" what's going on. People always ask him why he doesn't just listen to the game on the radio at home. He tells them, "There's nothing like a live sporting event." My parents, aunts, uncles, and cousins are devoted fans and watch every game. Being a Cincinnati fan is in my blood.

I knew every player on Cincinnati's team from playing pick-up basketball with them in the summers. I also knew the coaches. I've spent much of my life on their campus, so there wasn't much new for them to show me. When we did a scavenger hunt, I knew things the players didn't know. One of our tasks was to perform the Cincinnati fight song. None of them knew the words so I taught the entire team their own song! I felt at home because it wasn't much different than hanging out there in the summertime. This visit was fun, and I was always comfortable with the team.

My Ohio State visit was similar in that it was only an hour and a half from home and I knew everyone there as well. I had played AAU with or against most of the girls on the team. My host, Jessica Davenport, was a former AAU team-mate and friend, so we had a great time together. I loved Coach Jim Foster. He reminded me a lot of Coach Auriemma. I also had good relationships with the girls, and they seemed to be very close to each other. The facilities were some of the nicest I had seen. I don't think I could have gone wrong choosing either Cincinnati or Ohio State, but they weren't UConn.

My visit to UConn was with high school prospects Crystal Langhorne and Charde Houston. When I arrived on the outskirts of campus, the first thing I saw was cows. I couldn't believe it. "There are cows!" I exclaimed. "I don't know if I can do this." I was used to the University of Cincinnati's urban campus, so cow pastures were quite a surprise. Over time, I learned to appreciate these cows because they provided the main ingredients for UConn's famous Dairy Bar ice cream. As I saw more of the campus, I discovered an attractive mixture of classic, old buildings and more modern ones. There were beautiful lakes surrounded by trees with leaves of red and gold.

My first night, I had a great time because everyone was extremely friendly when we went out. My host was Diana Taurasi, who always made sure I was having fun. She was the best player in college basketball, but she made me feel like the most important person in the world. Everyone was incredibly welcoming, and I was included in every activity. The first hour of my trip confirmed what I already knew: I wanted to go to UConn.

The next day, we went to the Super Show, which is the first basketball practice of the year that's open to the public. There was a line wrapped halfway around Gampel Pavilion two hours before the doors even opened. When the festivities finally started, the arena was packed wall to wall. It was hard to believe the entire gym was full for a practice! I glanced across the court while the team was scrimmaging and noticed my name on a sign about 20 rows up in the stands. I shook my head and blinked my eyes because I thought I was seeing things. I looked again and saw fans holding "Mel" signs everywhere. I was shocked the fans actually knew who I was. A few years later, I ran into a fan who told me he printed a thousand signs with my name on them for that night. A thousand! He was a member of the Boneyard—a popular UConn fan website. The fan support was unlike anything I had ever seen. It was remarkable and definitely something I would enjoy getting used to.

The next day, I watched the team practice before I left. The structure of their practice was different from all the other schools I had visited. The intensity level was extremely high, and everything they did was precise. They all matched. They ran hard. They cut hard. They dove on loose balls. They talked and supported each other. Any time a player took a charge, the entire team ran over to pick her up. They worked incredibly hard, and I wanted to be a part of it.

On the weekend following my visit to UConn, I went to Duke. This was, by far, my worst visit. I was almost positive I wanted to go to UConn, but I continued with the visit to Duke, just to be sure. I went with an open mind because it's not fair to judge a place until actually experiencing it. However, once I got there, I didn't feel as welcome as I did at UConn. Soon after my arrival, my host asked me what other schools I was considering. When I mentioned UConn, she told me the whole program up there seemed kind of "weird." I'm not sure what that was supposed to mean, but it sure wasn't a good start to the visit.

I was at Duke during the weekend of Halloween. So, on Halloween night, we went out to Franklin Street, which is a huge event in Durham, North Carolina. The street was shut down, and thousands of people were walking the street in their costumes. This was a cool sight to see and the Duke team was having a great time together, but I wasn't included. I followed them, by myself, up and down Franklin Street. I wanted to hide and see how long it would take one of them to realize I was missing. I vowed, at that moment, to always make recruits feel welcome when I got to college. On recruiting visits, some schools make prospects feel like they are part of the program. Other schools often leave recruits feeling like outsiders—and that's how it was at Duke. They just didn't make a point of ensuring their guest had a good time. The coaches were nice, and the campus was pretty, but it wasn't the school for me.

When I returned home from Duke, I wanted to call Coach right away to tell him I knew UConn was the place for me. But first, I had to call the other schools I had visited to tell them my decision. I put off picking up the phone for as long as I possibly could, but I had to do it eventually. I called all three schools that same day. I had butterflies in my stomach before each call because I didn't want to hurt anyone's feelings. My parents assured me the coaches had been disappointed many times before. It was part of their job. After becoming really close with the entire coaching staff at the University of Cincinnati, I thought I broke Coach Laurie Pirtle's heart when I called to say no. I felt awful because all of her staff were great people and they couldn't have been more helpful. It was also hard to tell Coach Foster from Ohio State because we had grown pretty close. He asked if I wanted to think it over for a few days, but my mind was made up. Duke, on the other hand, was an easier phone call to make.

Before visiting Duke, I told Coach that I thought Connecticut was the right place for me, but I wanted to go on my last visit just to be sure. When I called Coach to tell him I would definitely come to UConn, I decided to play a little trick on him. After chit-chatting for a while, he asked about my visit to Duke.

I said, "It was so good. I had a great time."

"Well that's great," he said. "I'm glad you had fun."

"I don't think you understand. It was really good—like I think I want to go there good."

"What?"

"I loved it there; I think I want to go there!"

"Uh, well you just got back; you might want to think everything over."

"You know, I thought I was really gonna hate it, but I loved everything about it—the campus, the team. I love Coach G." (That's Gail Goestenkors, who actually was very nice.) "I just really think I'd get a better education at Duke. A degree from Duke is just so prestigious. I don't think I should pass that up. Before last weekend, I was positive I wanted to go to UConn, but I fell in love with Duke and I've completely changed my mind."

Of course, I was completely making everything up.

"I'm sure it was great, but you just got back. You should take a couple days to let it all sink in. Then we can talk about all of this again."

"I don't need any time. I'm positive Duke's the place for me."

Coach tried to convince me to think about it, but I kept saying, "I'm really sorry. I feel bad, but I think I wanna go to Duke." I dragged the joke out way longer than I should have, but I was having so much fun with it. When we were just about to hang up, I said, "Hey, one more thing."

"Yea?" he asked

"I'm just joking."

"What?"

"About everything. My visit to Duke was absolutely horrible. I want to go to UConn. I've known for a long time that I wanted to go to there."

"You little jerk! You little jerk!" he yelled, as I laughed hysterically. I thought it was the funniest thing in the world. That was the one time in my entire UConn career that I had the upper hand on Coach. He said, "You know, I have four years to get you back for this."

Official visit to UConn

To put this joke in perspective—a few weeks before, one of the top recruits in the country had withdrawn her verbal commitment to UConn and announced she was going to Maryland. Coach was devastated by that whole scenario so it wasn't very nice of me to play my joke on him. But I got him good—that's for sure.

The whole recruiting process is stressful for any kid. I was so thankful that my parents left the decision completely up to me. Many parents aren't willing to trust the judgment of a 17- or 18-year-old teenager. My mom and dad always made it clear they would be completely supportive of any school I chose, even though my mom wasn't a big fan of Coach Auriemma. She thought he was cocky, arrogant, and full of himself. She wasn't too far off, but that's what I liked about him. As a mother, she wanted me to go where she knew they would take care of her little girl. I can see why she didn't think Coach would be a heartwarming, lovey-dovey type. Still, she never tried to influence my beliefs throughout the process, and she had faith in my decision.

Other people had no problem giving me their unsolicited advice. I had at least a hundred people telling me a thousand different things. I was told to go here or go there, and what's wrong with this program, or that program. It was insane. I heard a thousand times that I wouldn't play if I went to UConn because I wasn't tall enough, I wasn't fast enough, and I wasn't athletic enough. But, ultimately, it was not about what everyone else thought. The only thing that mattered was what I believed, and I believed in UConn. I had confidence that not only could I make it there, I would excel. That's how I ended up at UConn. It was the best decision I ever made.

CHAPTER 3

Freshman Frustrations

SUNDAY, MAY 13, 2007

I took four courses during the spring semester. Now after only two days off, I start an intensive four-week Maymester class tomorrow. I can't believe this is my last summer here. My first three years have flown by faster than I ever imagined. I'm certainly looking forward to my senior year, but I wish I could slow down time. I don't know what I'll do when I have to leave this place. I've enjoyed every day I've been here—well, except maybe some from my freshman year.

When people think of UConn Women's Basketball, they think of winning and success, but my career at UConn didn't begin so gloriously. My freshman year was pretty rough. Ketia, Charde, and I were walking into an almost impossible situation. Our program was defending three consecutive National Championships. For each of the previous 10 years, UConn had had at least one First Team All-American guard. We were expected to follow in the footsteps of Diana Taurasi, the greatest player in the history of college basketball and two-time National Player of the Year. We had BIG shoes to fill, and we weren't ready for them. We didn't have the confidence, the talent, or the experience. The worst part was that we didn't realize how far we were from where we needed to be.

I was coming from a completely different world—high school basketball. Like all high-school kids, I thought I knew everything. As a top college prospect, I was the best player on my high school team, and I had the freedom to do almost anything I wanted. I went to the all-star events, like the McDonald's All-American Game. I was Ms. Basketball in Ohio. My team was undefeated and won the State Championship. I have never been a cocky or arrogant person, but

I started thinking I was good enough to do the exact same thing in college. However, once I got here, I realized I had a lot of work to do.

My first wake-up call came in the preseason with individual workouts. During these sessions, small groups of two or three players work on individual skills. My first workout was with senior guard Stacey Marron, and it seemed I couldn't do anything right. Everything was structured completely different from my previous experiences. Each time I passed the ball, I had to call out the name of the person I was throwing it to. I thought this was the most stupid thing I had ever heard. I did it, but with an attitude. I called Stacey's name loudly and obnoxiously, just to be a jerk. I thought, "What does saying some-one's name a thousand times have to do with shooting jump shots?" I didn't understand it then, but I eventually learned it was to teach us the importance of communication skills. The more a team talks to each other on the floor, the easier it is to play with one another. Now it's second nature to me.

My real frustrations began when I got a stress fracture in my foot just as full team practice started. I made it through conditioning, the hardest part of the year, but couldn't practice when it was time to play real basketball. According to the trainers, stress fractures are common injuries with freshmen because their bodies aren't accustomed to four hours of strenuous workouts a day. By the time I was healthy, I was a month behind in practice. I missed so much that I didn't know the offense. I was completely lost. It was much differ-ent than what I was used to. In high school, the plays were simpler, and if I went to the wrong place it didn't really matter.

Junior guard Ann Strother was the teammate who was always there for me, helping me adjust. I was confused with all the plays, so she tried to teach me where each player should be on the floor. We drew a court on paper and repre-sented the players with Starburst wrappers. I got really frustrated because I didn't know where any of them were supposed to go. Ann tried to take me seriously for as long as she could, but then she burst out laughing. I was on the verge of tears because I didn't know where to move a Starburst wrapper! After realizing how ridiculous the situation was, I joined in the laughter.

Later in the season, when everything was finally starting to make sense, I broke my nose. I had to wear a facemask for two months. This restricted my

The mask!

peripheral vision and caused me to have blind spots. This was a setback I just didn't need.

We started the season 8-4. In nine weeks, we went from being a top five team to number 16. The last time UConn was ranked that low was in 1993. Our disappointments came as a shock to everyone. When the year began, we weren't nearly as good as we thought we were. Our older players had won National Championships, but they had never been the leaders. They played in the shadow of Diana, who took over every big game. Morgan Valley and Maria Conlon didn't receive the same amount of credit, but they were extremely tough guys with strong personalities as well. Now they were gone, and we had to find some new leaders.

Coach knew from the first day that we were in trouble. One practice, he told us he didn't know how it was possible to have so many bad basketball players on the same team. He was accustomed to having the best players in the country, and we didn't match up to those standards. He told Ketia and me, "I used to have Sue Bird and Diana Taurasi, and now I have *you!*" He said since we obviously wouldn't be the most talented team, our only choice was to be the best conditioned. Sometimes when we couldn't do anything else right, we just ran. One day, we had a bad practice and repeatedly turned the ball over. Coach said, "I can't watch this garbage. I don't know how you guys don't go home every night and just kill yourselves!"

I just stared at him, thinking, "Did he really just say that?" We knew he didn't mean it, so we had a pretty good laugh when we returned to our dorm that night. I said to my teammates, "What if he found out I blew my brains out tonight, do you think he would feel bad?" I never told my mom those kinds of things. She already thought Coach was a bit of a psycho, so I didn't think it would help the situation. She always thought of me as her little girl, and she didn't want anyone to talk to her little girl that way. On the other hand, my dad thought it was hilarious. He got a kick out of Coach telling me I was the worst basketball player he ever coached. He understood it was all part of the sport and was meant to make me mentally tougher in the end.

There were many days that Coach got pretty frustrated trying to get through to us. He didn't think we deserved the privileges that good teams have, so he took everything he could away from us. He kicked us out of the locker room for two weeks. We had to carry our shoes in duffle bags and change in the hallway, like we were in high school. Our practice uniforms are usually washed for us every day, but we had to do our own laundry. He refused to give us any of our shoes or gear issued to us by Nike. We didn't get anything back until Coach felt we earned it. He told us nothing was going to be given to us just because we went to Connecticut.

Coach kicked people out of practice left and right. He sent Ketia to the pool almost every week. She can't swim very well, so that was the worst punishment he could give her. Charde always seemed to be running the stadium stairs inside Gampel. I only got kicked out of practice once. That day, there were four of us: Willnett Crockett, Barbara, Ketia, and me. He kicked the other three out for being lazy or having bad attitudes, but I was kicked out for being stubborn. He said I didn't listen and I wanted to do everything my own way. It was probably true, but I didn't think so at the time.

Coach told me every single day that I was sloppy. "You dress sloppy. You act sloppy. You play sloppy." I never remembered to tuck in my shirt, so Ashley Valley had to remind me every day before practice. I thought it was the most stupid rule I had ever heard. In the past, the only time I tucked my shirt in was for games. I wore knee-high socks and nail polish during games in high school. I learned early on that none of that would fly at UConn.

One day, Coach called me into his office because he heard a rumor that I wanted to transfer. He asked, "Someone told me you said if you weren't starting, you want to leave. Is this true?"

"What are you talking about?" I asked. "That might be the most absurd thing I've ever heard in my life." I never for a second thought about leaving. Still to this day, I have no idea where that information came from. I told him, "Coach, if I never play another second, I still wouldn't leave." I was in for the long haul, no matter how difficult the road was. My philosophy for the year was: *What doesn't kill you only makes you stronger.* I never gave up, and I never thought about transferring. I knew I'd get through it.

Ketia and I fought through our problems together. After losses, Ketia and I would vent for hours. We just sat in our room together and talked. We tried to figure out a way to make things better, but we didn't know what to do.

Was my life really that bad? I was getting a free education, free housing, free meals, and free sweats—just to run around for three hours a day. I met new people on campus each day and was experiencing a new and exciting life. I had 11 sisters who loved me, but I wasn't happy with the one thing I cared most about.

There was a period when I absolutely hated basketball. This scared me more than anything. For years, it was my love that drove me to be successful. Without it, I didn't know what to do. I went back to the place where I discovered my love for the game, in hopes that it would come back to me. Late at night, I went to the gym after a full day of practice. I spent hours upon hours in the empty arena, repeating the same drills from my childhood. It didn't take long for my love to return. It had been loyal to me for so many years that I knew it wouldn't desert me when I needed it most.

I wasn't the only one who was lost. Coach obviously didn't know what to do either. We finished with eight losses, which was equivalent to a losing season at UConn. Coach couldn't find a way to solve our problems. He benched some of us from time to time, hoping it would send us a message. I was a victim of this on a couple of occasions. I started a few times that year, but most of the time I came off the bench and played almost 20 minutes a night. I didn't know much, but I played hard enough that Coach liked having me on the floor. However, there were a few games when Coach got particularly frustrated with me and refused to put me in the game at all.

During the shootaround before the Tennessee game, we were working on breaking their press. The first time I touched the ball, I turned it over. Coach went ballistic. He told me I couldn't be trusted with the ball, and I wouldn't play a second. He wasn't lying. I must have been careless with the ball on the days leading up to the game. Still, I thought that was a little harsh for one turnover!

My worst experience getting benched was the North Carolina game. Again, I did something to irritate Coach and he told me I wasn't going to play. I guess it was better that he warned me every time, rather than it being a surprise!

My family came to the game with ESPN signs that said "Mel Thomas, Super Freshman," and I didn't play one second. They got more airtime than I did. I had friends from home call me and say, "Hey. I saw your mom on TV yesterday, but I didn't see you!" We lost the game.

When Coach walked into the locker room, he came directly for me and cursed me out. He said, "You do whatever you feel like doing. You don't listen. You don't pay attention." I looked at him, thinking "This man must be crazy. Did he forget that he didn't play me at all? How could this be my fault?" I really wanted to kill him that day.

Coach constantly tested my mental toughness. I had always been tough physically. Bumps, bruises, and floor burns never fazed me. My mind had always been tough enough to make my body do whatever I told it. I could handle pushing myself to run hard or to play through pain, but this was a different kind of mental toughness. Coach challenged me to believe I could do anything, even when it was beyond my abilities. I was being tested now against the best athletes in America, and one of the toughest coaches in the country as well. I had to learn to believe in myself more than ever.

I didn't realize how much confidence it took to be at the top. I thought I was confident, but Coach was exposing every doubt I had at practice. I thought he was such a jerk, and wondered why he was messing with my head. I started to question everything I did. I didn't even know when to shoot the ball. Shooting threes was my specialty, but I was reluctant to take even wide-open shots. One day at practice, I missed a few three-pointers in a row. Coach said, "Why are you shooting the ball? If you don't think it's going in, why shoot it? Don't take another shot the rest of practice." I didn't shoot again the rest of practice. Coach wanted me to have the confidence to say, "Screw you," and knock it in. I didn't understand then, and I wasn't yet confident enough to do that.

It seemed he knew exactly what was going on in my head. The days I was on top of the world, he usually left me alone. It was the days I was questioning myself and nothing was going right that he was on my case. All I wanted was for him to tell me I could do it. He could have said, "It's okay, Mel. You're great. You'll make the next one." That might have given me a little more confidence to hit the next one, but he didn't care about the next one. He was concerned with the shot I had to hit to win the Big East Tournament or to take us to the Final Four. He knew what was best for me in the long run, but it sure wasn't easy getting there.

It wasn't easy for our fans either. They had gotten used to UConn being on top, and when we weren't quite there, they didn't know what to do. Before I arrived at UConn, the team lost only four home games in 11 years. The fans went to every game, not *hoping* to see a win, but expecting one. After we lost to North Carolina, our coaches received an angry letter from one fan who said our team was an embarrassment to the program. She didn't think we had the heart, determination, and hustle of the Connecticut teams in the past, and that we weren't worth her time or money. She had purchased tickets to the Big East Tournament before the season started. After seeing us play, she no longer wanted to attend and believed she should be reimbursed.

Our coaches agreed we weren't worth watching, so they made us give the woman her money back. They took 10 dollars out of each player's meal money

All eyes on Coach Auriemma

44

in order to pay for the cost of the tickets. It was hardly a financial hardship for any of us because our meal allowance was pretty generous; but it wasn't about the money. Coach wanted to prove a point.

He told us, "When we were the best team in the country, everyone wanted to watch us play. It was like the circus was coming to town. People wanted to come see what all the buzz was about. Teams that couldn't sell a ticket would pack their arenas when we came to play. In a sense we've lost that. We've let it slip a little, and we have to find a way to get it back."

I wish this woman could have attended some of our practices and seen how hard we worked every day. Maybe she should have kept her tickets because we ended up winning the Big East Tournament.

Our team pulled together at the end of the year and played our best basketball of the season. Everything was finally making sense to me. After months of being stubborn, I started to understand my way wasn't working. I had to put my own interests aside and believe in the knowledge and experience of the coaching staff. My freshman year was extremely important to the development of my character.

Our season ended with a trip to the Sweet Sixteen. We finished about as well as we could have. Coach was often frustrated with us throughout the year, but he never gave up on us. Every day, he tried to convince us we were capable of accomplishing things we probably weren't capable of accomplishing.

The whole year was an eye-opening experience for me. It turned out to be a lot harder than I imagined. Some things were going to have to change if we wanted to get our program back on top. One thing that was sure to change was that Ketia, Charde, and I would become sophomores—and we'd have a much better understanding of our UConn program and the challenges of college basketball.

Our team got better with each passing year, and playing basketball became a lot more fun. My sophomore year, our record was 32-5, we won the Big East Tournament, and went to the Elite Eight. That year, I became a better listener and took the coaches' instructions more seriously. This helped me work my way into the starting lineup. At the end of the year, I received the award for the Most Improved Player in the Big East. My junior year, we went 32-4 and were undefeated in the Big East. But again, we were one game short of the Final Four. I have one year left to change that.

Me, Charde, and Ann

Charde (24), Nicole Wolff (21), Ann (43), Ashley (2), Ketia (11)

CHAPTER 4

"Brasil! Brasil!"

WEDNESDAY, MAY 16, 2007

Tomorrow I leave for Colorado Springs to try out for the United States Pan American team. When my invitation came in the mail, I was a little surprised. Going into my senior year, I had never been asked to play for a USA team before. My only experience with USA Basketball was during my junior year of high school at the USA Youth Development Festival. This was a five-game tournament at the U.S. Olympic Training Center in Colorado Springs. Fifty of America's best prep players were divided into four teams that competed for a gold medal. I have never had the opportunity to play for a team that traveled the world to compete against other countries. Watching many of my UConn teammates play for USA Basketball deepened my desire to be a part of it. The youngest teams compete in an Under-18 age group, so even some high school players get invited. I'm almost 22 years old, so I was shocked that I finally was asked. I'm really excited for this opportunity. Charde played for a team immediately after she graduated from high school, and she is trying out again this year with me.

The tryouts are being held at the Olympic Training Center in Colorado Springs, which is an unbelievable place. It has facilities for just about every sport imaginable, where United States athletes train for the Olympics and other international competitions. I'm a little nervous about trying out. Almost all the girls I'm competing with have played for USA teams in the past few years. What if I go all the way out there and get cut? The committee will select two teams— one is an Under-21 team that will compete in the World Championships, and the other will play in the Pan American Games in Brazil. Because of my age, I am only eligible to play for the Pan American Games. Fifty people are trying out, and only about half will make the first cut.

THURSDAY, MAY 17, 2007

There is no way I'm going to make this team. I played horribly today, and I couldn't make a shot. I played hard, doing all the little things I usually do, but I don't know how important those things will be to the committee. I want to make this team so much, but I don't know if it will happen. When I got into the shower after practice, my frustrations leaked down my face as the water washed away my tears. I gave it everything I had, but I wasn't getting the results I wanted. I still have four more practices left to redeem myself. I'll just keep playing my hardest.

SATURDAY, MAY 19, 2007

I find out tomorrow morning if I advance past the first cut. We've had double sessions each day for the past two days. I'm exhausted, but I feel much more confident than I did my first day here. I've been playing better, and hitting a lot more shots. I have made a point to do all the little things they teach us at Connecticut—diving on loose balls, talking on defense, supporting my teammates, and running the court as hard as possible. I'm hoping my hustle will set me apart from other people with a similar skill level. I guess I'll find out tomorrow. The committee is cutting each team down to 16 players, and then four more will be cut in July when the teams reassemble in Washington, D.C., for practice. I did everything I could, but I'm still nervous. All I can do now is wait.

SUNDAY, MAY 20, 2007

Today, everyone had to report to the gym at 8:00 in the morning. We sat along the walls, waiting to hear some kind of announcement. I think they were trying to torture us, because it seemed like we were there for hours! Some people were much more relaxed than others. A few knew they had a spot and were laughing, carrying on, and having a great time. Others, like me, were so nervous we could hardly breathe. Finally, they called us into the center of the gym. If our name was not read, we were to leave the gym immediately. The list was in alphabetical order, so I had to wait for *T*—almost at the end of the alphabet. The Rs and the Ss went by so slowly, and my stomach got tighter and tighter with each name. Then, finally, I heard it: "Thomas." I had never been so excited to hear my name in my life! When they finished reading the names, those who were cut started walking toward the door. Many of them were completely devastated. I felt sorry for them for a minute; but more than anything, I was just glad it wasn't me. After they cleared the gym, we met our teams and were fitted for our gear. I was incredibly happy, but it wasn't over yet. We still wouldn't find out for another month and a half if we made the final team. I said to myself, "I've come this far, and I'm going to find a way to make it to Brazil."

MONDAY, JUNE 11, 2009

It's been a few weeks now since tryouts. I've been working out at school to get ready for training camp. I always train extremely hard, but I'm determined to be in the best shape of my life for these tryouts. The 16 remaining girls are all great players, so the second cut is going to be even harder than the first. Not only am I working out, but also I'm taking a couple of summer courses. We usually take at least six credit hours in the summer in order to lighten our load during the season.

The new freshmen, Lorin Dixon and Maya Moore, are on campus taking classes as well. Lorin reminds me a little bit of Ketia her freshman year. She is extremely quick, but doesn't quite know how to use her speed yet. She can't shoot very well, but she is constantly working on it. The first thing I noticed when we played pick-up was that she can jump out of the gym. One time, I thought I had a wide open layup because Lorin was a full step behind me. I didn't think that little girl had any chance of blocking my shot, so I jumped up thinking it was uncontested. Well, I sure was wrong! Lorin leaped three feet in the air and pinned my shot on the backboard.

Maya is the sweetest girl in the world and is an incredible basketball player as well. Her work ethic impresses me more than anything. She's competitive, plays extremely hard, and is always in the gym. She has the potential to be good, really good. I'm excited to play with both of them this year.

We have known Maya for only a few weeks, but that is long enough to learn how much she loves food. However, it hasn't been enough time to know that today was her birthday. Renee found out around 10:00 p.m. and quickly spread the word. All the stores were closed, except one convenience store that's open 24 hours. Renee left in search of cake mix, but returned with about 15 Twinkies. "That's all they had!" she said. We whipped together a cake of Twinkies, glued together with icing. We invited Maya over to our apartment and everyone sang Happy Birthday as we huddled around the Twinkie cake. It was a mess, but Maya's eyes lit up. She was ecstatic and couldn't have asked for a better birthday gift.

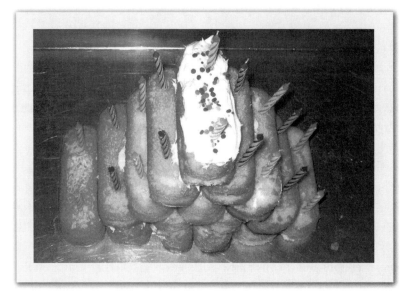

Maya's Twinkie birthday cake

FRIDAY, JULY 6, 2007

I finished summer school just in time to come to Washington, D.C., and resume training with USA Basketball. I'm going to do everything in my power to make sure I earn one of the 12 spots for the Pan American Games. We had practice tonight at the Washington Mystic's practice facility. It's much different to practice with new players and a completely new coaching staff. I'm very comfortable with the way we do things at UConn, so it will be a challenge to learn new drills and different plays. I am so accustomed to our system it has become second nature to me. I really like the coaching staff, which consists of Dawn Staley from Temple University, Bill Gibbons from Holy Cross, and Kathy Delaney-Smith from Harvard. I might finally get to play for Coach Staley after all!

SUNDAY, JULY 8, 2007

We find out tomorrow if we are part of the team. We've had "two-a-days" the past couple of days, which included *a lot* of running. I think Coach Staley has been testing us to see who is tough enough to survive. I've pushed myself to the limit, so hopefully I showed that I have what it takes. I've practiced pretty well, but I have no idea if I'll make the final cut. I have one last night of tossing and turning before the team is announced.

MONDAY, JULY 9, 2007

This morning, each player had set appointments, scheduled five minutes apart. We each went into a room one-on-one with Sue Donohoe, the chair of the USA Basketball Women's Collegiate Committee. It was like elimination time on a reality TV show. I walked into the room and sat down on the chair in front of her. There was a long, dramatic pause, and then she would either say, "You *will* be traveling with us to Brazil," or "You will *not* be traveling with us to Brazil." She looked me in the eyes, and I thought I was going to pee in my pants. "You *will* be traveling with us to Brazil."

I'm so excited! I made it! The rest of the team includes: Matee Ajavon (Rutgers), Nicky Anosike (Tennessee), Jayne Appel (Stanford), Marissa Coleman (Maryland), Emily Fox (Minnesota), Alexis Hornbuckle (Tennessee), Charde Houston (Connecticut), Tasha Humphrey (Georgia), Erlana Larkins (North Carolina), and Angel McCoughtry (Louisville).

THURSDAY JULY 12, 2007

I'm still in Washington. We've been practicing long hours since the team was announced because we only have a few days left to prepare before we leave for Brazil. This morning we went to George Mason University for the United States

Proud to wear the USA jersey

Olympic Committee processing. First, they showed us a slide show of past American athletes who competed for their country. As I watched it, I was mesmerized by the thought that I would soon be in the same situation. I grew up watching the Olympics and although this is not the same, I still have the opportunity to represent my country. I will do this with enormous pride.

We learned about the Pan American Games and the culture of Brazil. The Pan-American Games began in 1942 and are held every four years in the year preceding the Olympics. The Games officially start tomorrow on July 13, but we don't leave for a few more days. Thirty-six different sports will be involved, with more than 5,000 athletes from 42 countries competing.

We went through medical screening and then received our apparel. They gave each of us a laundry basket, and we gathered items until our baskets were full of socks, shoes, hats, t-shirts, and warm-ups. It felt like Christmas!

We had practice later in the day. It's not easy having a three-time Olympic gold medalist point guard for a coach. Taking care of the ball is of the utmost importance to Coach Staley, so she made us run for each turnover we had. It seemed like we were back on the line with every other play. Practice is tough, but the coaching staff assures us that fighting through it is the way to the gold.

FRIDAY, JULY 13, 2007

Today was an unusual day for us because we didn't have anything scheduled until our scrimmage at 4:30 against the Under-19 team. They are coached by Doug Bruno from DePaul, Cynthia Cooper, and Carol Owens. They are training to compete in the FIBA World Championship in Bratislava, Slovakia. Maya Moore is on the team, so I was able to spend some time with her. Coach Auriemma was there watching, and I gave him a big hug after we finished. He said, "Oh, so you want to talk to me now, huh?" I just started laughing.

"The first thing you do when you find out you made it is call CD, not me."

"Well that's because CD checks up on me. She called the night before final cuts and told me to let her know as soon as I found out. So, yes, I'd rather talk to CD than to you."

Of course, he had to come back with a smart comment, saying, with a laugh, "Well, when you want playing time next season, call CD." I wouldn't expect anything less than a sarcastic reply from Coach. He's a Philadelphia smart aleck, so we have to have thick skin and have fun with it. Coach has a playful, joking relationship with all of his players. He says, "If you can't make fun of the people you love, who can you make fun of?"

SUNDAY, JULY 15, 2007

Tonight both teams went to the WNBA All-Star Game. After the game, we walked back to the bus. Cynthia Cooper was with us when a fan caught sight of her. "It's Cynthia Cooper!" she yelled. Within 10 seconds, she was mobbed by a group of adoring fans. She's indisputably one of the biggest names in women's basketball, but she took time to smile, converse, sign autographs, and take pictures with every single fan. Whether she wanted to or not, she gave each fan her undivided attention. I was very impressed with how down to earth she is. She is an incredible role model. She's always having fun, making jokes, and dancing. She's very playful and friendly, but it's easy to see what a competitive nature she has. When she's coaching, the fire in her eyes and her will to win are always evident. I feel so privileged to be around both her and Coach Staley. They have accomplished almost everything possible in their sport. They have won multiple Olympic gold medals, had successful WNBA careers, and are now great coaches. The amount of knowledge they have is incredible, so I am trying to soak up everything I can from them.

Everyone is extremely excited that we leave tomorrow for Brazil. When we first arrived in Washington for training, we didn't think this day would ever come. It was a little intimidating to look at a practice schedule that showed two practices each day for two weeks straight, but we finally made it.

MONDAY, JULY 15, 2009

We stopped at the Holocaust Museum on our way to the airport. This was an incredibly powerful experience, and was difficult to witness. When we arrived, we each received a booklet depicting the life of a child who lived during the Holocaust. As we walked through the exhibit, which progresses chronologically, we read along in the book to discover what the child's life was like at that point in the Holocaust. My child survived, but many did not. One part of the exhibit was filled with hundreds of shoes, which were taken off before people went into the gas chambers. Many of them were extremely small—obviously children's shoes.

A theatre showed videos of survivors discussing their experiences. One lady's story was so powerful it sent a chill through my spine. When the Nazis forced the Jewish people into concentration camps, her father instructed her to put on her snow boots in the middle of summer. She didn't know how her father was aware of what was to come, but his anticipations were right. She walked in the snow for three winters in snow boots, while many other girls wore sandals. She believed she survived because she could run through the snow when other girls could barely walk. She recalled watching young girls snapping off their toes like twigs because they were dead from frostbite. Everyone has learned how horrific the Holocaust was, but actually seeing it in front of my eyes made it much more realistic. It was an extremely moving experience, and I left feeling thankful for the life I have.

TERÇA-FEIRA JULHO 17, 2009

Olá from Brazil! We flew through the night and arrived in Rio de Janeiro this morning. Our trip from the airport to the Athletes Village was far from what we expected. The area through which we drove was extremely poor. The buildings were completely run down and covered with graffiti. Shoeless children were playing soccer in the streets or on basketball courts. Brightly colored clothes were hanging outside each living area, adding color to an otherwise dreary scene.

When we arrived at the Athletes Village, military police, armed with large rifles, were everywhere. The Village is absolutely gorgeous, a complete contrast to the devastation we saw on the way here. The Village consists of 17 different colored towers, two of which are occupied by athletes from the United States and Barbados. The towers surround a small lake, and infinity pools are placed so that each is shared by a few different towers. On the bottom floor of each tower is a computer lab accessible for athletes who want to contact home. In this room, the events and games are on television so athletes and coaches gather around to watch their countrymen compete.

After we got settled in our rooms, we walked to the cafeteria. The international center sits directly across from the cafeteria and has a huge Jumbo Tran that displays live events from the Games. The international center boasts a variety of amenities, including a place to exchange U.S. dollars for Brazilian reals, souvenir shops, and a dance club. In the cafeteria, we had trouble communicating with the Brazilians who served our food. We couldn't speak their language, so we had to point to the foods we wanted. I felt kind of rude, but I did it with a smile, so hopefully that counts for something. Smiling is a universal form of communication!

We had our first practice this afternoon in a small, hot gym. The nets were made of thick pieces of rope braided together, and soccer lines were painted on the court, in addition to the international basketball lines, which are different from ours. The international lines have a wider lane and a deeper three-point line. Soccer goals sat behind the end lines under each basket. When we arrived, the Argentinean women's team was practicing. We had to stretch and do warm-up drills outside because we were scheduled for only one hour on the court.

After practice, we had a meeting with other United States athletes to warn us of security risks. One of our athletes and his parents had been robbed at gunpoint earlier that day. We're supposed to travel in packs and not wear USA gear outside the village because it makes us easy targets. The Brazilians are not very welcoming to Americans. We are booed at almost every venue.

Following the meeting, my roommates and I took showers, which was an experience to remember. There was no hot water for the first few days. It wasn't even lukewarm; it was ice-cold. First, we were all standing there in our towels and we'd say, "Is it hot yet?" Someone would stick in a finger or toe and scream, "No!" When it still didn't warm up after a few minutes, we figured ice-cold was our only option. I finally got in, but I refused to immerse my whole body because it was too cold. I got damp by cupping water in my hands, and then I turned off the faucet while I washed with soap. When I finally rinsed, Charde was laughing hysterically as I attempted to move under the water. I just wanted to wash the suds off my body, so I could get out of there as fast as possible!

Next, it was Charde's turn, and my time to laugh. She attempted to wash using the same tactics I did. "Make sure you call me when you rinse!" I yelled, because I wanted to get a good laugh watching her be as miserable as I had been. When the water hit her back, she screamed; and I shrieked with laughter. We were both out of control until we realized that people who were competing the next day were trying to sleep, and we needed to shut up!

QUARTA-FEIRA, JULHO 18, 2007

When we walked into the gym today for practice, we noticed birds flying over our heads. Tasha Humphrey said, "Well, this is the first time I've ever shared a gym with pigeons." There was no air conditioning, and it was too hot to keep the doors closed, so the birds just came and went as they pleased. There are definitely some new experiences down here!

After practice, Coach Staley called a team meeting. She talked about the importance of leadership on our team. She said, "We have to make sure we all stick together. No matter how many minutes you play, we're all in this together. We're in foreign territory with everyone against us, so we only have each other to depend on. During the games, there are going to be times when everything won't always go right, and we need to have people we can count on to smooth things out. I think we need to figure out who these people are going to be. What qualities do you think are important for your leaders to have?" We established that our leaders had to have high energy, positive attitudes, and the ability to motivate their teammates. We voted for the players we thought would best lead and keep our team together. I voted for Matee Ajavon and Candice Wiggins because they are both point guards who do a good job running the team. They play with great intensity and can take control when necessary—directing and encouraging their teammates. Apparently, this was the general consensus because Matee and Candice were the two selected by the team.

Later in the day, we scrimmaged against Brazil. We were stretching when they walked into the gym. They were a little intimidating because they were all huge, grown women. One player was 6'9"! They looked much older than us, like they were in their thirties. They wore sleeveless tops and spandex shorts that said Brazil across their butts. Not only was their look unusual, but also their style of play. Some of them played slowly and awkwardly, but they were very efficient. They were experienced and knew how and when to cut. They didn't do anything fancy, just simple moves. The scrimmage was close the entire time, but we ended up losing by four points. I think it was good for us because it showed us we had some work to do if we wanted to win the gold medal.

SEXTA-FEIRA, JULHO 20, 2007

Today we had a team breakfast before heading to the gym to play our first game against Columbia. Before the game, we lined up by number and traded gifts with the other team. We traded small USA basketball pennants for Columbian pins. Our starters were Matee Ajavon, Candice Wiggins, Alexis Hornbuckle, Tasha Humphrey, and Nikki Anosike. They blew the game open, and we won 95-41.

Tasha was interviewed after the game, and the communication barrier between languages became apparent. The reporter asked, "How you feel Columbia is such a horrible, pitiful, low-level team?" That's probably not exactly what he meant, or maybe they are just much blunter here. Tasha kind of chuckled and answered the question the best she could. Our next game was against Argentina, so the reporter wanted Tasha's opinion of them. As if the first question wasn't bad enough, he asked, "Do you think Argentina is as horrible, pitiful, low-level team?" Again, Tasha responded and gave the most politically correct answer she could.

Later, we watched the first quarter of the Jamaica/Brazil game. When Brazil ran out in their yellow spandex, the entire building erupted in applause. It was the most energetic crowd I had ever seen. Everyone was cheering and dancing. When we left the stadium between quarters, the whole crowd booed us.

SÁBADO, JULHO 21, 2009

Today we had shootaround in the morning, and then occupied our time by going to the mall before our game at 7:45. We played Argentina, and they were extremely aggressive—to the point of playing dirty. They had three flagrant fouls during the game, but we won 85-54. I played a decent game, scoring nine points in 17 minutes.

DOMINGO, JULHO 22, 2009

Tonight we beat Cuba 78-63, but it was a closer game than the score revealed. We were down early in the game, but made a run and stayed in command the rest of the way. I didn't play at all, and neither did Emily Fox, who had 18 points the night before. They were a very athletic team, so I guess Coach Staley didn't think we were athletic enough to play in the game. I'm really sick of people telling me that I'm not athletic enough, but it's not about me. My team is 3-0, and we're two games away from a gold medal. I'm here representing my country. If that means cheering my teammates from the bench, then that's what I'll do.

SEGUNDA-FEIRA, JULHO 23, 2007

Our next game was against Canada, and we won 75-59. I came off the bench and played really well, scoring 10 points in 15 minutes. After the game, Coach Staley pointed out to my teammates how admirable it was that I played so well after not getting in the game yesterday. She said that's a really hard thing to do.

I felt great after the game. Although I was disappointed about not playing the day before, I didn't let it affect me. I had two choices: pout about it or come back stronger, and I chose the second. Sometimes players have to sacrifice what they want for the good of their team. Yesterday, I took on the role my team needed, which was to support them from the bench. Today, it was my time to shine. The overall achievement of the team is much more important than anything that has to do with me. Winning and celebrating with my teammates is what makes everything worthwhile. With that win, we moved on to play in the championship game against Brazil. The United States hasn't won the Pan American Games since 1987. Our hard work has brought us right where we want to be—in the gold medal game.

TERÇA-FEIRA, JULHO 24, 2007

For all of our games, the crowds have been fairly small, just a few thousand people. The big crowds roll in whenever Brazil takes the court. During our warm-ups, I could see all the fans piling into the stadium. They were the craziest fans I've ever seen. Some wore costumes—angels with wings, inner tubes and flippers, and even Fred Flintstone. It looked like a Halloween party! They wore tights and brightly colored wigs, and almost all of them were waving Brazilian flags. From the court, all we saw was yellow, green, and blue in the stands. They sang and danced and cheered much louder than I have ever heard. "Brasil! Brasil!" chants echoed through the stadium.

I didn't play at all, so I was incredibly nervous on the bench the entire game. It was much different watching than playing because I had no control over the outcome. I sat next to Emily at the end of the bench, and I never let go of her arm the entire second half.

We battled Brazil back and forth the entire game. We trailed by one at half-time, and by four approaching the fourth quarter. With 3:27 left, we led 65-62.

Then Tasha made a three, followed by a layup by Matee, and we never looked back. We pulled it out, winning 79-66. Matee decided to be Superwoman and took over the game in the fourth quarter. Everything she threw up went in, and she finished with 27 points.

Running onto the court to meet my teammates after the game was a great feeling. We did the impossible—beating a very experienced Brazilian team in their home country. When we stepped onto the podium, I can't explain the feeling I had. I was so proud to be an American. Brazilian women in beautiful gowns handed us flowers, and we kissed both cheeks of the man who placed the medals around our necks. I sang along as our National Anthem was played, but I could barely hear it as the Brazilian fans chanted over the music. I thought that was rude, but it didn't ruin the moment. I got a little teary-eyed as I looked at our flag flying atop the pole. This was a dream come true for me.

We went to the club inside the Village when we got back. People from many different countries were partying together, dancing to music in a language most people didn't understand. The differences in culture were very apparent in the unique styles of dance. It was packed wall to wall, so it felt like I was dancing with six people at the same time. I was completely drenched in sweat, but it was so much fun. We met people from many different places. Nearly all the athletes traded their gear with players from other countries. I couldn't believe my amazing experience was over. I developed great relationships with some of the girls, and I didn't want to leave. I am so thankful to everyone who gave me the opportunity to be a part of it.

CHAPTER 5

From Home to Home

It's been a few weeks since I returned from Brazil. I traveled home to Cincinnati to spend time with my family and friends. Tonight, I went to a surprise party to honor my high school coach, Scott Rogers. After six years at Mount Notre Dame High School, he's stepping down as the head coach. His third year coaching, we won our school's first State Basketball Championship. He's been to the State Championship game every year since, and won two more titles. Coach Rogers' current and former players hid behind a door, waiting for him to arrive. When he walked through the door, we yelled, "Surprise!" His jaw dropped, and he stood there dumbfounded for a long time. He got a little teary-eyed and hugged everyone in sight. There was a ceremony with an open microphone, so any of the players could reminisce about Coach Rogers. It was great to see old friends and to remember the good times we had together.

I discussed my first encounter with Coach Rogers. My freshman year of high school was a terrible experience. It was the only time in my life my team finished with a losing record. We were 10-11. Before the beginning of my sophomore season, my team was in the library waiting to meet the new coach who had been hired. This perky, goofy-looking man with a bald head ran in with a sign that read "Columbus." He looked at us and said, "So what does this mean to you?" We looked at each other, thinking, "Who is this crazy man?" No one said anything, but he kept asking, so we figured it wasn't a rhetorical question. My best friend, Ali, guessed, "Ummm…the capital of Ohio?"

"No, not quite," he responded. We had no idea what this little game of his was. He finally said, "This is where the Final Four is, and this is where we are

Celebrating Mount Notre Dame High School's 2004 State Championship

going this year." I was thinking, "This man must have lost his mind. Does he not know that we had a losing record last season?"

Although we didn't end up going to the Final Four, or winning the State Championship that year, it was what we worked toward every day. Our hard work was rewarded the next year when we finished with a record of 23-3 and established ourselves as one of the best programs in Ohio. In my senior year, Coach Rogers' vision came true. We had a perfect season (28-0) and won the State Championship. No matter how unrealistic it seemed, Coach Rogers thought we could do anything. He had great confidence in his abilities as a coach and in his team. This confidence definitely rubbed off on us. I knew we were the best team, and I felt we were invincible. When we were playing, I was always the most confident player on the court. The day Coach Rogers took over was a blessing because I learned so much from him. He was hard on me every day, and that set the framework for what I would soon experience at UConn.

Photo courtesy of Rick Elliott

Nothing could ever completely prepare me for the transition to college, but I was confident that I could do anything; it was just a matter of time.

Coach Rogers was more than just my basketball coach. In my sophomore year of high school, our team went to a training camp at Purdue University in Indiana. After diving for a ball during a game, I once again found a piece of my tooth missing at the expense of the floor. As I had done before, I went over to the scorer's table, set the tooth down, and went back in the game. Every time I ran up and down the court I could feel the air pierce the exposed nerve of my tooth. We still had more games to play, so something needed to be done. Since my coach was a dentist, he bonded my tooth right there in the hotel room. He did a pretty good job because my teeth look great, and nobody knows they aren't originals.

TUESDAY, AUGUST 14, 2007

I don't have to go back to school for two more weeks. I decided to drive two hours to visit Ann Strother in Indianapolis where she plays in the WNBA for the Indiana Fever. Ann likes her teammates, but the whole environment is completely different from college. In professional basketball, everyone lives their own lives and playing the game becomes a job. When people play for money, their attitudes change. Ann said, "It will never be the same as playing at UConn. I feel like my best basketball days are over." More than ever, I want to cherish my senior year at UConn.

It was great to see Ann because she has been an amazing friend to me. I latched on to her pretty fast when I first arrived on the UConn campus. I was lost, and she was a great role model to show me the way. She's an even better person than she is a basketball player. Whenever I needed her, she'd drop everything she was doing to help me. My freshman year, if I was upset or homesick, she'd say, "Come on. I know what will make you feel better. Let's go get a Slurpie." I'd jump in her car for the 10-minute ride to 7-11. I'm not sure if it was the Slurpie or if it was Annie talking with me, but I always felt better when we got back.

TUESDAY, AUGUST 28, 2007

During my time at home, I have been working out with my favorite trainer, Sherwin Anderson. He has been a huge inspiration in my life. When I was 15

Working out with Sherwin Anderson

years old, I was playing basketball with some high school teammates at Xavier University. My friend Ali found a large, playground ball in the gym and thought it would be funny to throw it at me, like we were playing dodge ball. She threw the ball at my feet, and I tried to leap over it. Instead, I landed directly on top of the ball and twisted my ankle. A stranger from across the gym ran over to make sure I was all right. His name was Sherwin Anderson. He was a personal trainer who had played basketball at Xavier. There was a reason we were brought together that day. We shared an incredible passion for the game and formed a lifelong bond.

Sherwin is able to motivate me more than anyone else I have ever met. He wants me to get better just as much—if not more—than I do. I have had some truly remarkable people help me to grow as a basketball player. They have each taught me something different that I have carried with me through-out my career. Sherwin was the first person to really focus on my individual skills. He expects nothing but the best, just like Coach Auriemma. When I do shooting drills, he only counts shots that swish through the net. If my task is to make 100 shots, and I do, but 50 nick the rim, I still have another 50 to shoot. When we first started working together, Sherwin often challenged me with new drills I had never seen before. I couldn't do a lot of them, and they frustrated me to death. I would trip and fall over my own feet. Nothing came easy. Workouts that were supposed to take an hour took me two or three. I always wanted to stay in the gym until I finally got everything right. Sometimes Sherwin would kick me out of the gym, and I would go to another gym until I mastered the skill.

Besides my parents, he has been the most influential person in my life. I fell even deeper in love with basketball the day we met, and that hasn't changed. I called him complaining every other week my freshman year, and he was always there to tell me to suck it up. "It's great to be great," he would say. "That's what you are, so go out there and do what you were born to do." He helped me through so many tough times that I could never repay him for everything he's done for me.

WEDNESDAY, AUGUST 29, 2007

Today, I arrived back in Connecticut. I'm happy to be here again, but I had a great time at home. It's nice to have a change of scenery. During the year, I'm lucky if I make it home for Thanksgiving, Christmas, and a few weeks in the summer. The rest of the time, I'm at UConn, working out and taking classes.

THURSDAY, AUGUST 30, 2009

Today is Brit's birthday, so I put birthday signs all over campus. I searched for the worst pictures of her I could find and made them into obnoxious birthday posters. One showed her shoving an entire meatball into her mouth in one bite. I placed them on every telephone pole from our apartment to Gampel. I also posted them all over the gym, locker room, and student union. When she saw them, she claimed she wanted to kill me, but I think she secretly liked it.

We had a meeting with Coach this afternoon to talk about our preseason schedule and the upcoming year. At Connecticut, there is a rule that all freshmen are required to be in study hall regardless of their academic achievements. When we're sophomores, we can be released from study hall if our grade point average is above 3.0. Coach called out Meghan and Kaili in front of everyone in the meeting. They are both pretty smart, but hadn't worked hard enough in the classroom, so Coach made sure everyone knew it. He said, "It all goes hand in hand. You're either a hardworking individual or you're not. You can't pick and choose when you want to work hard. If you're lazy in school, it will carry over onto the court." Coach has always been big on balancing academics and athletics. It means just as much to him that we achieve as well academically as we do on the court. It's an expectation for us to have a strong work ethic in everything we do. We may not hear about the

Happy Birthday, Brit!

academic side as much, but if we're not doing what we're supposed to be doing, Coach gets all over us.

MONDAY, SEPTEMBER 3, 2007

Today we had a "Welcome Back" party at Coach's house. Coach and Mrs. A (his wife, Kathy) welcome us into their home for dinner all the time. Coach cooked chicken on the grill for us, and it was really good, as usual. All the players are extremely close to Coach's family. They're our family away from home. They have been supportive and welcoming since the first day I set foot on campus.

Coach is far more enthusiastic about this year than I've ever seen him. While we were at his house, he pulled Renee and me off to the side to talk about the upcoming year. He's counting on us, as captains, to lead our team in the right direction. He told us, "You two need to figure things out, and the less stuff that comes back to me, the better. If you guys feel like something is out of your control, and you need my help, let me know; but the rest is on you." He gives a lot of trust to the people he thinks can run the team. He's not out there on the court with us, so we need to be the ones who take control. He thinks our team is finally good enough to go all the way.

Coach wanted to get a feel for how the team was coming together and asked how the freshmen were fitting in. We told him Lorin is unbelievably quick and that Maya's been really good in pick-up games. We have all five starters back from last year, so he said it would be great to bring Maya off the bench. Coach loves when he subs and our team gets better, while the other team gets worse. In practice, the blue team and the white team scrimmage every day. The starters play for the blue team, and the subs make up the white team. Some of the best Connecticut teams in the past have had such talented second teams that they often beat the starters in practice. The first four people coming off the bench this year are Maya, Ketia, Brit, and Kaili. No other program in the country has the depth we have. Coach said, "Look, if we don't win a National Championship this year, I should be fired." I'm really excited about his attitude for the start of the season because I have the same expectations. He's done this before, so if he's that certain about our chances to win, it makes me that much more confident.

CHAPTER 6

27 Ways of Death

TUESDAY, SEPTEMBER 4, 2007
DEATH: DAY 1

Preseason conditioning starts today. The preseason is the worst time of the year for basketball players. It combines running, lifting, and speed training. I've been through three already, but it doesn't get any easier each time. Preseason shows which players are mentally tough and who can push themselves past their point of exhaustion. We know once we get through it, we'll be much stronger when the season begins.

Preseason running is awful. I've seen my fair share of people throw up, pass out, and just about everything but die! A few years ago, we had to do a workout called the Gauntlet, which consists of two 400-yard sprints, four 200s, eight 100s, and sixteen 40s. After we finished the 100s, Barbara Turner thought we were finished. She stepped off the line to grab her water bottle. Coach West, our strength and conditioning coach, said, "Oh you're not finished; you still have sixteen 40s." Barbara was so surprised she threw a silent fit like a little kid. She didn't say anything; she just punched and kicked the air for about 10 seconds. She looked like a crazy person! I guess that's what exhaustion can do to you. I wanted to laugh, but I was so out of breath I couldn't. Barbara got back on the line and finished the workout; but I'll never forget that little tantrum. It was one of the funniest things I've ever seen.

That might be a normal workout for someone who runs track, but I'm a basketball player, so it wasn't easy for me. In cartoons, stars always appear over the characters' heads when they get hit. Well, that day, I was so delirious I literally saw stars.

I push myself as hard as I can every time we work out. I've learned that everything we do is only as hard as we make it. In the weight room, we have the choice to challenge ourselves by adding weight, or we can be content taking the easy road. On the track, if we're only giving 80 percent, it's going to be a whole lot easier than if we go all out. Our success, not only as individuals, but also as a team, depends on every one of us striving to be our best. If we are satisfied giving less, then we can't complain when things don't go our way later in the year.

The Gauntlet was a bad experience, but nothing compares to the time we had to do punishment runs. Before my sophomore season began, four of us went out one night and did something stupid; and the whole team had to pay. I didn't start the problem, but I didn't stop it either, so that made me guilty too. Our whole team usually went out together, but everyone else was home for the weekend. When our coaches found out, I thought my life was over. We had a meeting with the entire coaching staff, and I never felt so embarrassed and ashamed. We were all afraid of what Coach was going to do to us. In addition to our regular workouts, our entire team had to wake up and run at 6:00 in the morning for more days than we want to remember.

I thought our teammates were going to kill us. They weren't even on campus, and they had to run for our mistake. I didn't blame them one bit. I would have wanted to kill me, too. I don't think there was anything we could have done or said to remove the death stare from their eyes, but after every sprint, I'd say, "I'm so sorry, guys." After running three miles, we had to run up Cemetery Hill for what seemed like a hundred times. The hill is located in the middle of a cemetery and one trip up and down is a half mile. It feels like it goes on forever. We knew it was a bad sign when Nicole Wolff, one of the best-conditioned athletes on our team, puked at the top. Tahirah Williams had it the worst. Going uphill, she pushed herself so hard that she was swerving like a drunk driver all the way down—dry-heaving every 10 steps. The only thing I could do to help rectify the situation was to win every race. If I made my teammates run, I'd better give it everything I had.

This was by far my worst experience at UConn. I have never felt so bad for anything I've done. I wrote Coach a three-page letter saying how sorry I was, and God only knows what else. I rambled on and on because I didn't know what else to do. I wonder if he still has it. It would be pretty funny to see. We all laugh about it now, but at the time, it *definitely* wasn't the least bit funny.

WEDNESDAY, SEPTEMBER 5, 2009
DEATH: DAY 2

Preseason workouts are always at 7:00 a.m. Our classes are scheduled in the morning because we have afternoon practice. On alternate days we swap 1:30 and 4:30 practice times with the men's team. During the off-season, we play pick-up and lift weights during the afternoon at these times.

Today's conditioning was a long-distance run. In addition to our team, Tonya, Jamelle, and two of our managers, Matt Gade and Vinny Bruno, ran a 3.2-mile loop around campus. It was our first time running this loop this year, so it was hard to find the right pace. I was in a rhythm until we hit the last hill—then I thought I was going to die. However, I found a way to push through it and finished first alongside Vinny, with a pack of Matt, Kalana, Tahirah, Lorin, and Maya trailing shortly behind. Everyone else came in one by one until Kaili was the only one left. We do everything as a team, so everyone jogged back to finish the run with Kaili. She showed a lot of heart by sprinting through the finish line. It's always much easier to do something difficult when we have encouragement and support from our teammates

After I finish a workout, I often wonder how I pushed myself through it. Conditioning is completely mental for me. There have been so many days when I didn't want to run, but I always convinced my mind otherwise. I'm able to do what I hate because of what I love. I imagine that each thing I do will determine whether or not we win the National Championship. I treat each sprint or rep in the weight room like it will be the difference in the tournament.

SATURDAY, SEPTEMBER 8, 2009

The first week of preseason is finally over! Each day, we alternated between running the three-mile loop and running sprints. That's in addition to playing pick-up, doing individuals, and lifting. Now we are lucky if we can walk.

I'm so excited that I survived this week, but my body is extremely tired. To limit the soreness in our bodies, our whole team soaks together for 10-15 minutes in the cold pool after training. We immerse ourselves chest deep in 50-degree water. This is absolute torture at first, but after the first few minutes, it's not so bad because our bodies get numb. This suffering is worth it, though, because we feel so much better when we get out.

MONDAY, SEPTEMBER 10, 2009
DEATH: DAY 5

This morning we ran long-distance in the rain. Before preseason started, Coach told us all the coaches were going to run with us every morning, but we sure haven't seen him run a step. I finished first. I get mad if anyone beats me, so I do everything possible to finish in the front.

I've been extremely competitive for as long as I can remember. When I was a little kid, I often played board games with my blind uncle, Roger. One day when I was 11 years old, we were playing Candyland. My uncle was ahead the whole game, but he got stuck trying to draw the last card to win the game. After I caught up to him on the board, we both needed a purple card to win. On my next turn, I picked an orange card, but I told him it was purple. He saw right through my little scam, "Are you telling the truth?" he asked.

"Of course," I responded. He had just beaten me three games in a row, and I wasn't about to lose again.

"Are you sure?"

"Yea," I lied. I was so competitive that I lied to my blind uncle about a game of Candyland. I felt really bad about it, so I said a prayer later that night. Still, I'm probably going to Hell for that one.

SUNDAY, SEPTEMBER 16, 2009

We decided to celebrate making it through the first two weeks of Hell, so we went to a party last night. I was in the car with Kaili, and we drove up the same hill that we had been running three times a week.

I said, "I'm so happy I'm not running this hill right now!"

"Did you have to run this hill before I got here?" she asked.

I looked at her, confused, "You're joking, right?"

The perplexed look on her face told me she definitely wasn't joking.

"Kai, we run up this hill every other day."

"No, we don't."

"What are you talking about? We run this route three times a week." Her face dropped, and I started laughing hysterically.

"Kai, where have you been running!?"

"I never ran this way before! I was so far behind everybody else I couldn't see which way to go! I swear I thought I was going the right way!" I laughed about it for a good 15 minutes. She had been running the wrong route for two weeks!

MONDAY, SEPTEMBER 19
DEATH: DAY 10

This morning when my alarm clock went off at 6:30, I felt like I had only been sleeping for 20 minutes. When we walked outside, it was freezing. I could see my breath all the way to the gym. It's only September, but the temperature is already in the 30s some nights. I'm from Cincinnati, so I'm used to cold weather, but still, no one wants to run in it.

Our team, coaches included, ate breakfast together at the dining hall after the workout. We do this frequently in the off-season. Our coaches think it's important for us to have relationships off the court as well as on. Coach once asked Barbara in the locker room, "How many brothers and sisters does Kalana have?" She didn't know the answer. Coach said, "Do you guys have real relationships with one another or do you just pretend? This is your family—the people you trust with your life. You better know every single person inside and out." My teammates are my best friends, and we do everything together. We work out together, live together, and go out together. I don't know how much closer we can get. The best thing is that we always have fun.

After breakfast, I headed back to the gym for my individual with Tonya, who coaches the guards. I have two a week—one on Mondays with Jacquie and one on Wednesdays with Maya and Kalana. Today, I worked on shooting off screens. Coach told me I need to improve on reading my defender, so I can do a better job getting open this season. Next, we both shot threes for five minutes straight while the managers recorded our makes and misses. I shot 74 for 96. The rest of my day was filled with lifting, pick-up games, and more classes. I was so tired after workouts that it was hard to concentrate on anything else. During my evening classes, my eyelids were heavy, and my head kept nodding as I struggled not to fall asleep. I survived my management lecture, and then had to go straight to marketing class. I'm so tired now, and I still have homework to do for an 8:00 class in the morning. I hate my life!!

College athletes' lives are very different from those of regular students. Many regular students go out three to four nights a week. Our schedules are so busy that we don't have time for much except classes, study hall, workouts, and practice. It's like having a full-time job. Once athletes sign a letter of intent, they give up a lot of the freedom that normal students have. It's a choice we make for something we love. I can't imagine my life any other way. I have friends at UConn who don't play sports. Sometimes I have visited them in the afternoon after I had already attended three classes, practiced and lifted—and they would just be getting out of bed. "What do you guys do all day?" I asked. "Oh, this," one of them replied with remote control in hand, "I didn't feel like going to class." "Not feeling like it" is not an option for us. We have to be aware that each one of our actions affects 13 other people. If we don't want to go to class or work hard, we let down not only our coaches, but also our best friends.

THURSDAY, SEPTEMBER 20, 2007
DEATH: DAY 13

Our pick-up games are completely different this year than they have been in the past. They haven't been this competitive since Morgan and Maria were here. They both stayed on campus for an extra semester to take classes and finish their Bachelor's degrees. They were always in the gym, working out with the younger players. The summer before I started school, Morgan and Charde got into a fist fight playing pick-up. They were guarding each other in the post, and it became more and more physical with each play. Words were exchanged on a couple of trips down the court; and then, before we knew it, they were squared up to fight one another.

That was the mentality that Morgan played with; she treated each pick-up game like it was the National Championship. When she lost, she'd be ticked off the entire day. I can't count the number of times the ball ended up in the stands at the expense of Morgan's foot. No matter what it was, she refused to lose. One time, Morgan, Maria, Diana, and some of the football players decided to play a *friendly* match of the word-guessing game, Taboo. The score was tied, and Morgan had to give clues to make her teammates guess for the winning point. They didn't get it right, and Morgan was a *little* upset. She stormed out into the hallway with her fists clenched. We thought she was going to break something, over a stupid game of Taboo! Winning was everything to Morgan and Maria, and that's probably why those players ended up with three National Championships. They were the most competitive group of people I've ever been around.

Pick-up now reminds me a great deal of how it was when those guys were here. The games are so competitive that we fight every day. We play games to seven—counting normal baskets as one point and three-pointers as two points. There is an argument about the score in just about every game. At some point, we have to stop and individually count our points because there's a discrepancy with the score. There are obviously no refs, so the offense has to call their own fouls. That can get pretty ugly as well. If we don't start playing some other opponents soon, we're going to end up killing each other. It's a good thing, though, because it shows how much everybody wants to win. There have been some incredibly intense games over the past week. Just yesterday, Charde and T got into it. I thought Charde was going to punch someone again, but we stopped the fight before anybody's nose got broken.

In the summertime, we usually play against the football players, but they are in season during the fall. I think it helps to play against guys because in general, they are bigger, stronger, and more athletic. That doesn't mean they are better, but it forces us to raise our level of play. Most girls who make it to the Division I college level grew up playing against boys. It makes us stronger and quicker, while teaching us to be smarter. The same moves we typically do against girls may not work against the guys. We have to find ways to outsmart them, rather than overpower them. It's fun to play against different opponents because we get tired of beating up each other all the time. We win some games, but the guys beat us as well. Many of them played basketball in high school and are pretty skilled.

The only way we can beat them is by playing together and using our basketball knowledge to outsmart them, like making the right cut or pass at the right time.

Every time new football players come to play us, they have a tendency to be a little reserved at first. The veteran football players try to warn them, saying, "Play like you would against a dude. They're not regular girls, I'm telling you." But the new guys never listen. We usually take a commanding lead before they realize how good we are.

FRIDAY, SEPTEMBER 21, 2009
DEATH: DAY 14

At the crack of dawn this morning, we ran 100-yard sprints on the football turf. After we finished, Coach told us he was pretty happy with our effort so far. "Every Championship team I've ever coached had the instinct to treat everything like it's the most important thing in the world to them. I'm finally starting to see that from this group, but we're not 100 percent there yet." Coach is never satisfied. He always thinks there's room for improvement.

MONDAY, SEPTEMBER 24, 2009
DEATH: DAY 15

I'm getting so used to running that it doesn't seem too bad anymore. I feel like I'm in really good shape now. Coach West records our times for everything we do so we always have new goals to beat. The workouts are geared for continuous improvement, so we reach our peak fitness when practice starts.

One of our managers, Stacey Nasser, put me through a workout today. We have about 12 managers each year, so at each practice, every player has her own. The basketball office receives pages and pages of applications each year, and there is a long process used to select new managers. The head managers interview the applicants, asking about previous basketball experience and their reasons for wanting to be a part of our program. After these interviews, the applicants are narrowed down, and then on court tryouts are held. The applicants are tested on rebounding and passing drills, their ability to take stats, and their overall interaction in the environment.

Another manager, Stacey Gordon, told me that when they cut people, they feel they're shattering dreams. They receive angry emails, saying, "I'm sorry you didn't realize my potential. I could have added a lot to the program, but you never gave me a chance." A few days ago, I met a student who was trying out to be a manager. She came all the way from Maine with a dream of being part of our basketball program, but she was turned away. Most people probably don't realize there is tough competition even to be a manager at UConn.

Our managers and practice players are a huge part of our program. They take every practice just as seriously as our players do, spending as much time as we do in the gym every day. They do it for the sheer love of the game because nobody sees all their hard work. Each year, we have about five practice players who come to practice every single day. I don't know how they do it, because they get stuck doing all the dirty work. Sometimes they play defense 98 percent of the day, and they get yelled at by the coaches just as much as we do. My freshman year, we had a practice player who was extremely physical and recklessly fouled our players. He was completely out of control. Our coaches were afraid he would hurt someone, so they kicked him out of practice. Still, he came back every day watching from the bleachers, until they finally let him return.

After my workout, we went to Coach's annual golf tournament, called Fore the Kids. The event supports the Connecticut Children's Medical Center. We worked a basketball station set up to raise money for charity. The golfers paid five dollars to shoot for raffle tickets. They could either shoot the ball themselves or ask one of us to shoot for them. My teammates volunteered me as the person for the job. I guess they were smart, though, because out of 50 shots, I only missed one.

A few golfers challenged Maya, Kaili, and me to a game of three-on-three. It wasn't our typical game because we were all dressed in khakis and polo shirts. One of the golfers even wore his golfing glove during the game. We were joking around at first, but then all of a sudden a couple of their shots went in, and the score was two to two in a game to three. We began playing seriously, and Maya passed me the ball as I was coming off a screen set by Kaili to knock in the game winner. A friendly game turned out to be a little more competitive than we expected, but it usually happens that way. After we were off duty, we drove golf carts around the course. There were 13 of us piled into three carts intended for two people each. T and I hopped on the back, though there was nowhere to sit. We had to squat with our legs interlocked to keep from falling off. It would have been just great if one of us had to miss the season due to a golf cart injury!

WEDNESDAY, SEPTEMBER 28, 2009
DEATH: DAY 19

Yesterday we had to run "stadiums," which are never fun. There are 100 steps in our old football stadium, which I know because I count them every time I climb to the top. We ran 10, which, by far, isn't the most we've ever done. My sophomore year we were challenged as a team to run 200 stadiums. There were 10 of us, so we could divide them up between us. The idea was that 200 could never be done individually, but we could accomplish anything together. Some people picked up the slack for others who struggled. I ran the stairs 22 times, and my legs felt like they were going to fall off. When I stopped, my legs were shaking uncontrollably.

This morning, we had our one-mile test on the track. Coach says the timed mile isn't a test of fitness at all. If he wanted a true sense of our fitness levels, he would make us run 10 miles. He said, "Anybody can run around a track four times, but this test is a measure of willpower and heart to see how far you can push yourself."

I ended up finishing at the head of the pack in 5:57. After I crossed the line, I was watching Kaili run her last lap on the opposite side of the track. I ran across the field to finish it with her. I wanted to see if I could push her to run a little harder. She completely sprinted the end of the run. Last year at this time, there was no way in the world she could have run that fast.

Kaili reminded Jamelle a lot of herself when she arrived on campus. Jamelle has been her biggest cheerleader, but also her harshest critic. She wants to see Kaili succeed, so she was extremely proud of her effort today. When Jamelle was a freshman, she was out of shape and needed to lose some weight. She ran the mile in 9:18. By the time Jamelle was a senior, she had cut three minutes off her time. Coach made fun of Jamelle, saying, "Pam Webber probably finished, went and got a glass of orange juice, came back, and you still probably weren't done."

After we finished, Coach told us we were one of the fastest groups he's had. I had been dreading running the mile all week, so I was greatly relieved when it was over. For once, Coach was finally satisfied with something we did...or so I thought. His excitement about our times quickly turned into determination that we could run it faster. He informed us that we had to run it again in two weeks, and everyone had to beat their first time. I was furious. Former player Svetlana Abrosimova holds the record at 5:45, and he said I had to beat it. I went as fast as I could the first time, but I'll try my hardest.

TUESDAY, OCTOBER 2, 2007
DEATH: DAY 21

I had an accounting exam today, so I've been in the library for the past two days straight. The only times I left were to work out and sleep. My brain felt like it was about to fall out of my head. I'm a bookworm when it comes to school. I put just as much energy into school as I do into basketball, but it's much harder to do it for school. I love basketball, so it comes naturally. It's more of a struggle to excel at something I don't enjoy. I hate school, but I hate being bad at anything more than I hate school. I'd rather put in the extra time and know that I gave my best. I obsess over getting good grades as much as I'm obsessed with excellence in basketball. I'm capable of getting a 4.0, so that's what I expect. My grades usually aren't *quite* that high, but that's what I strive for every semester.

Today, we had to fill out our bio page for the media guide. One of the sections asked for a list of our hobbies. T was sitting next to me while I was filling this out. I asked her, "What hobbies do I really have besides playing basketball and hanging out with you guys?" T said, dead serious, "Well, studying. You like to study." "T! No I don't! Who likes to study? I study because I have to!" She responded, "Well you're always studying. I figured you liked it!" I study so much that people think it's my pastime and hobby!

I guess it's worth it because it shows up in my grades.

SATURDAY, OCTOBER 6, 2007

Yesterday morning, I woke up at 7:15 with absolutely nothing packed. We traveled to Burlington, Vermont, this weekend, for Ashley Valley's wedding. Ashley was a senior point guard when I was a freshman. She married her college boyfriend, who played on the men's basketball team. We were supposed to leave by 8:00, but nothing ever goes as planned. I couldn't even get Brit out of bed until 8:30, and she still had to pack. We finally got on the road about an hour later than we anticipated. We had to pick up our former teammates, Nicole and Ann, from Boston. Since we didn't know exactly where Nicole lived, we got very lost. It shouldn't have been a shock because I have the worst sense of direction of anyone in the world. We eventually just parked, and Ann and Nicole had to find us on foot!

After that little detour, we were on our way. Well, somewhat—we didn't know the location of the hotel or the church. We just headed to Burlington in hopes we could locate the place eventually. Four hours and a lot of laughs later,

Me, Brit, Nicole, and Ann at Ashley's wedding

we finally found the hotel. We mooched our way into Jessica Moore's room, who was also a senior when I was a freshman. We were running late, so four of us had to use one shower and be ready to go in 45 minutes. Surprisingly enough, we made it to the church on time. Ashley looked beautiful, and Diana, Morgan, and Jessica were her bridesmaids.

The reception was a blast. The whole bridal party changed into white Nike sneakers that had Mike and Ashley's names and the date embroidered on the side. They didn't change out of the dresses or tuxedos, just the shoes. I've never seen a bride and a groom in sneakers, but that's Ashley for you. We danced with Mrs. A and some of the other administrators from UConn. It was funny to see some of these people out of their element.

I went to say "hi" to Coach, and somehow that turned into a full-blown conversation about basketball. We were at a wedding, not at the gym! Coach started to get all sentimental on me. He said, "You're such a huge part of this program. With the team we have right now, we don't have anybody to replace your work ethic. I hope the younger guys will step up and work as hard as you do, but you can never count on freshmen. They're just too young and don't know anything."

That was a huge compliment coming from Coach. I said, "I want all that hard work to pay off, Coach. I want to be good this year, really good."

"You can do anything you want to do. The only limitations are the ones you place on yourself. You're not tall enough, you're not quick enough, but with the way you play, no one would ever know. Imagine what you could do if you were Ann's height, or even Dee's height. But you're not, so you have to work with what you've got. You can overcome that by being the most confident person on the court."

I agreed and said, "Coach, we are really going to win this year."

He responded, "It's up to you older guys. I expect a lot more out of players when they get to be seniors. With certain guys, there's not much I can do or say that can rattle them. They just want to win, and they'll do whatever it takes. I think you can be that person this year. Every really good senior who has come through this program has had the confidence to do that. They've run the team, not me."

I was deeply moved by how much trust and responsibility Coach was giving me. I was on the verge of getting too emotional, so I had to end the conversation and go back to the party. By no stretch of the imagination is it normal to cry about basketball at a wedding reception, so I had to get away. I'm a big softy when it comes to things I truly care about. I know it's only October, but I want so much to win.

After the reception, we all went out in Burlington. It was great to hang out with all my old teammates. I hadn't seen those guys in a long time, and I really missed them. But tonight was just like old times.

We returned to the hotel late that night, where six of us piled into Jessica's room. Nicole and Brit slept on the floor, using towels as blankets. It was the most disorganized trip in the world, but that didn't stop us from having a great time!

TUESDAY, OCTOBER 9, 2007
DEATH: DAY 26

It's almost over. We have only one day left of preseason. The past two days have been testing days. We test regularly to measure how much we improve from our training. Yesterday, we maxed out in the weight room, which means we determined the highest amount of weight we could lift for one rep for various exercises. Today, we did the 40-yard dash, the vertical jump test, and the beep test. The 40-yard dash is a sprint. Electronic eyes record our times at 10 yards and 40 yards. My time was one of the slower ones on the team, but it was as fast as my legs would take me! The vertical jump test measures the difference between the standing reach and the height reached at the top of a vertical jump. I wish I could jump 36 inches like Lorin, but I can't. My vertical leap was the second worst on the entire team. My athletic ability isn't the best in the world, but I find ways to get around it. Some people can get away with slacking off a little because their 90 percent is faster than my 100. The way I see it, I have no choice but to give everything I have on every single run.

The beep test is one of those drills that I can win by outworking everyone else. It's a test of maximum aerobic fitness and simple guts. Every time we see Coach West walk onto the court with the boom box, we prepare ourselves. This test involves continuous running, back and forth, between two lines 20 meters apart. We begin running when instructed by the CD in the boom box; and we have to reach each line before the next beep sounds. At the start, there is a lot of time between the beeps, so we only have to run at a slow jog. Over time, the beeps get closer and closer together, and we have to run faster and faster. Eventually, players are unable to keep up with the pace. When a player misses two beeps in a row, she's eliminated. The beeps get relentlessly closer together, forcing us to sprint as fast as we can. My teammates kept dropping out one after another, until I was the only one left. I have won every beep test I've competed in since I was a freshman. It's not because I'm fast, but because I refuse to give up. I usually run until I'm light-headed and dizzy.

WEDNESDAY, OCTOBER 10, 2007
DEATH: DAY 27

Today was the final day of my last preseason. We had to run the mile again, and we were challenged to beat our time from two weeks before. Everyone beat their time, except me; and mine was exactly the same. Lorin and I were running together in the front of the pack until she started to pull away. Trying to keep up with her, I ran a much faster first lap than normal because I didn't want to lose. Coach West called out our first split at 1:09, which meant we were on pace for a 4:36 mile. This is a minute and 20 seconds faster than I can run. I was so tired after the first lap that I struggled to recover for the rest of the race. I could have done much better if I had paced myself more intelligently. I wanted to stay in front, but it ended up hurting me. When I crossed the finish line, I literally fell. My legs just gave out and I dropped to the ground. Coach ran over, "Are you okay?" Everyone thought something was seriously wrong with me because I was on the ground hyperventilating, but I was just that tired. Lorin broke Sveta's record, finishing in 5:35. I had won every single long-distance run for the entire preseason, but I lost to a freshman on the very last day! I give her credit, but I'm still mad.

CHAPTER 7

Practice Makes Perfect

FRIDAY, OCTOBER 12, 2007

Each year, this weekend is a huge event in Connecticut because it's the start of basketball season for both the men's and women's programs. The hysteria is more intense than usual because our fans have been eagerly waiting for months to see their Huskies back in action. They can't wait to cheer on the returning players, and they're even more excited to check out the new freshmen. The fans know all about them, but haven't seen them play yet. Recruits are always on campus to see the festivities. It's interesting to look at these high school juniors and seniors and think that four years ago I was in the same position.

This year, the men's Midnight Madness and our Super Show are on the same evening. According to NCAA rules, teams aren't permitted to practice until a certain date. Many men's programs have their first practice at midnight on the first allowable day. Our Super Show has traditionally been the next day. However, our school has combined the two this year, calling the event "UConn Basketball's First Night." Until the arrival of the Connecticut Sun in 2003, there were no professional sports teams in Connecticut. Therefore, UConn Basketball has been embraced by almost all sports fans in our state.

For our team, all the lights were turned off, except for one spotlight. Smoke shot in the air as each player was introduced one by one and had her own time to shine. Like a Broadway star in the spotlight, each girl showed off her best dance moves. The fans loved it. After everyone was introduced, Coach addressed the crowd. He said, "Some years, you just have a special feeling about a team, and this year I do, and we really hope to share that with all of you."

After Coach's talk, we had a shooting contest. Each of us was partnered up with a fan from the stands, and we took turns shooting. I got the luck of the draw because my partner was pretty good, so together we took the title. Next, our coaches split us into two teams (blue and white) and we had a 10-minute intra-squad scrimmage. After we finished, the men's team had their player introductions, a slam dunk contest, and then a scrimmage.

The most amazing thing about First Night is how many fans come for this event. It's always close to a sellout—with nearly 10,000 people cheering for us in Gampel Pavilion. There are only a handful of women's college basketball teams who draw that large a crowd for their biggest regular season games. This night is more about entertaining our fans than having a serious practice. This is the only time of the year when we get to dance, joke around, and be show-offs. Before our regular games, we are all business. Coach doesn't believe in doing anything fancy. He prefers we entertain by playing great basketball.

Coach wants us to always look professional and take pride in our appearance. We wear team shoes, matching socks, no sweatbands, no tattoos. We don't have our names on the back of our jerseys. At UConn, what's important is the name on the front of our jerseys.

Renee showing off her moves at the Super Show

MONDAY, OCTOBER 15, 2007

It's only the third day of practice, but Coach isn't satisfied. He doesn't question our talent, but he's not yet sure if we are tough enough. He said, "We don't have enough competitive guys yet to win a National Championship. Too many guys are okay with finishing, as long as they don't finish last. Then we got other guys who kill themselves every time they're on the court.

"You can tell a lot about a person's character by preseason conditioning. Everyone could see how competitive Mel is from the beep test. She hates to lose at anything, whether it's sprints or a drill. Lorin's a competitive guy, too. You can see that by her mile time. Until we get everyone on that level, we're not there yet. Once you guys want to do every little thing right, then we'll be really good. Until then, we still have a lot of work to do."

So back to work it is.

SATURDAY, OCTOBER 20, 2007

Last night, my teammates and I went to our football game. UConn's football program is on the rise. They moved from Division I-AA to Division I only five years ago, and they've made huge strides since then. They finished 8-4 my freshman year and won the Motor City Bowl. This was the first bowl appearance in school history. Today we played Louisville and overcame a 10-point deficit in the fourth quarter to win 21-17. All the students rushed the field after the game, and we were no exception. Everyone laughed as we watched T run full speed at the football players, tackling them to the ground!

After the celebration died down, the players made their way back to the locker room, and the security personnel started forcing the fans back into the bleachers. Instead of following everyone else, I was looking for a little excitement. I said to T, "Let's run to the other end zone!" Of course, T agreed, because she's always up for doing something crazy. When we crossed midfield, we saw five security guards running toward us. By the time we reached the end zone, the guards were trying to snatch us up, and threatening to arrest us. I was laughing so hard and was so out of breath from the sprint that I could barely breathe. A football field is a whole lot longer than a basketball court! CD probably wouldn't have been too happy with us because she's very adamant about representing our program with class. But we have to have a little fun sometimes, right!?

WEDNESDAY, OCTOBER 24, 2007

We have been practicing for 10 days now, and it's been great so far. Coach is different this year. He's more optimistic and more cheerful than I've seen him before. He knows we're good enough to go all the way. In the huddle today, Coach said, "Before practice each day, we have to come in thinking we're not good enough. I know you're good. You guys know you're good. And so does everybody else. But the minute you guys come into practice thinking you're good is when you stop improving. We're not good enough yet; but if we keep working, we will be when it's time."

Coach strives for perfection, and he's never satisfied until he reaches it. That's why he has five National Championships. He drives himself crazy trying to get the best out of us. The past couple of years, our best hasn't been good enough. He's worked his butt off and done everything in his power to change that. He was used to having the best players in the entire country and accustomed to winning. My freshman year, we lost eight games, which equaled his total losses from the previous four seasons combined! This year we're back where we want to be, and he's a happier and better coach.

One of Coach's best attributes is teaching his teams to think like smart basketball players. Coach shows us how to see things on the floor: how to cut, when to cut, and what's going to get us open. He always tells me it doesn't matter how athletic I am. If I'm smarter, I'm better. That's why Connecticut teams have been so good in the past. They've not only had the best players, but they were the smartest ones as well. Looking back, I feel like I knew nothing when I first started here. Coach teaches us how to play basketball, rather than just run plays. The drills we do in practice teach us how to read defenses and react. The right movements are drilled into our heads until they become second nature. I've gotten much smarter, but there is always more to learn.

Today, Coach, Renee, Tina, and I went to New York City for the Big East Conference's Media Day. A limo picked us up from practice, and the four of us piled in for the three-hour ride. Each team brings their head coach and a few players to represent their university. Tonight, all the players had dinner at the Hard Rock Café. When dinner ended, the three of us walked over to thank the Big East representatives for the meal and for organizing the evening. Most of the other players left without thanking their hosts.

Coach always stresses having good manners, and being grateful for what people do for us. My first year here, someone held the door for us at a restaurant, and Coach watched every single person walk by without saying "thank you." We're usually very polite, but with all of us talking and carrying on, it must have slipped our minds. Not one of us was aware of our lack of courtesy until later that night when Coach addressed it, and we saw how disappointed he was in us. "People take their time to do something nice for you, and you don't even appreciate it," he said. "Don't ever think you're above saying 'thank you' for all the small things." Coach always finds a way for us to learn from everything we do. We realized how important it is to show true kindness and appreciation that night. Since then, I have made a point to thank every person who does something nice for me and remind my teammates to do so as well. We say "thank you" to Coach every time we go out to dinner, to our bus driver when he picks us up, to people who hold doors for us, and to anyone else who offers a nice gesture.

When Charde and I were in Brazil, we were usually the only ones to thank our coaches for dinner. They said, "You can tell what program you're from. They teach you girls right up there at UConn." It's really a tribute to Coach, and to the type of person he is. Everything he believes is important in life, he stresses in his program. He wants us to have respect for others and to be genuinely good people. Also, he expects us to have a sense of pride in the way we carry ourselves and the way we represent our program. We aren't allowed to dress sloppy, wear headphones in public, or use our phones at team dinners. All these things earn respect for our program and for each one of us as individuals.

Although Coach receives most of the credit, all of our coaches play significant roles in establishing our team values. Coach may be the boss, but CD does a lot of the detail work. She's usually the one that keeps everything running smoothly. She makes sure everyone is following the rules and is polite and respectful. CD has been by Coach's side since their first day together at

UConn. From the very beginning, they laid a foundation for what they envisioned the program could be. They worked toward it every day until they finally reached it, but even then they didn't relax. If any UConn team gets complacent, they risk letting our best traditions slip away. So, we never get complacent. We do things the right way *every* time, which is why our program has been consistently strong for the last two decades.

Walking down the street on the way back to our hotel, I realized the people around us weren't very friendly. Tina is from New York City, and she told Renee and me that no one says "hello" to one another. She said, "If someone said 'hi' to me when I was walking down the street, I would look at them like they were crazy and keep moving. I would think they wanted something from me."

"Yea, right." Renee and I didn't believe her. "In West Virginia, everyone says 'hey, how you doing?' when they see someone, whether they know them or not."

"No, definitely not here."

I didn't believe her, so I argued, "I bet someone would say 'hi' to me if I said 'hello' to them."

"Try it. I bet they don't."

Renee and I attempted to make eye contact with every single person that walked past us so we could say "hi." Tina laughed as person after person ignored us. We found one person in about 30 that acknowledged us. New York City's just a different place, I guess. I don't know any other city like it.

Later that night, when a bellhop brought our bags up to the room, Tina answered the door. He carried our bags inside and stood by the door, staring at Tina. Tina said, "Alright, thanks," and shut the door in his face. Renee and I were laughing hysterically because he was obviously looking for a tip, but Tina had no idea. We opened the door, offered him a tip, and apologized for our clueless friend.

THURSDAY, OCTOBER 25, 2007

At the Big East meeting, all the coaches had an opportunity to address the crowd. Coach said, "We have a chance to win a lot of games this year because we have really good guards. Tina's been doing really well, too. Yesterday at practice, she got an offensive rebound that wasn't her own miss, and she almost blocked a shot." Everyone laughed. We can always count on Coach to be a comedian. We were ranked number one by every single coach. Maya was chosen as the Preseason Freshman of the Year, and Renee and Tina were named to the Preseason First Team.

SATURDAY, OCTOBER 27, 2007

Yesterday, the lights went out during practice. It was in the middle of 11-man break, which is a drill everyone hates. It's a full-court, three-on-two drill. We have five minutes to score 25 points against the defense, counting by ones and twos. If we don't reach the goal, we have to run. If we do reach it, we still have to run…just not as far. I got really excited, thinking we wouldn't have to finish the drill, but I sure was wrong. When everyone stopped, Coach said, "What are you doing? I didn't tell you to stop!" We could barely see, so the ball was flying everywhere. We finished the drill and ran our sprints in near darkness—like nothing was wrong.

After practice today, we had a shooting competition from half-court. Maya and Kaili have a ritual in which they shoot 100 free throws after practice and then make a half-court shot before they leave. Today, Coach and I got in on the action. Coach shoots underhand with one hand, like he's bowling. Surprisingly enough, it goes in more often than one would think. The contest was a race to see who could make the first basket. Kaili won, followed by Maya, and then Coach made one before me. I wanted to retire from basketball! It was pretty embarrassing.

WEDNESDAY, OCTOBER 31, 2007

Today is Halloween. Our manager, Justine Durr, dressed up as CD for practice. Everyone is aware of CD's idiosyncrasies, so it was hilarious when Justine imitated them. First of all, during practice, she's constantly squatting underneath the basket. When she's not there, she's always yelling, "Sharper cuts!" "Touch the line!" or "Run harder!" Not a day goes by that we don't see CD with a Diet Coke in her hand. Justine wore a short, poufy, blond wig, had her shirt tucked in like CD, and mimicked everything she does.

Last year, for Halloween, all the players wore spandex to practice. We tucked our jerseys into them, and I busted out the face mask from freshman year. Coach wore baggy pants, a gold chain, and "cool" sunglasses in an attempt to be some kind of gangster. CD taped Smarties candies to her sweats and became "Smartie Pants." Jamelle and Tonya dressed as the "Black Eyed Peas," wearing shirts with the letter P and drawing black lines under their eyes. All the coaches have a serious side, but they know how to have a good time as well.

THURSDAY, NOVEMBER 1, 2007

Tomorrow, we play an exhibition game against the USA National Team with Sue Bird, Diana Taurasi, Lisa Leslie, and many other great players. It will be our first real test to see where we stand. It's strange to play against so many of the players who were my heroes when I was growing up. I have a picture of Lisa Leslie and me when I met her at an autograph signing in a Cincinnati mall.

Towering over Lisa Leslie

I was 10 years old and thought it was the greatest thing in the world. I never imagined then that I would someday play against her; but now, she's just another player standing in the way of what I want to accomplish.

MONDAY, NOVEMBER 3, 2009

We played the game yesterday and lost by 16. At halftime, Coach cursed out Tina because she had only one rebound. In the second half, Lisa Leslie blatantly beat her down the court and got a wide open layup. Tina didn't play again the rest of the game. Coach approached her on the sideline and said, "You're doing the same thing on the bench that you did in the game." In basketball, there are some things players can control and others they can't. Running the floor is something players can control, and that's why Coach was so angry.

It was hard to play against those guys because they are all so experienced. I thought we were pretty smart, but playing against them showed that we have a long way to go. They knew what cut to make and when to make it, and there wasn't much we could do about it. We were also playing against three former UConn players—Diana Taurasi, Sue Bird, and Swin Cash—who knew our system and many of our plays. During the game, we had the ball on the baseline, and Maya called a play from out-of-bounds. Sue said to me, "Man, you guys still run this play?" She knew exactly where I was going to cut and beat me to the spot. So, we had to make adjustments as the game progressed. Playing against such a great team exposed our weaknesses and opened our eyes to what we need to work on.

Diana and Sue have come back to UConn to practice with our team a few times since I've been here. Diana is the most confident person I've ever played against. In one of the drills, we had to guard them one-on-one. Diana thought she would score every single time, and usually she did. I was on defense once when she had the ball.

"Do you want me to go to the right or the left?" she asked

I gave her a dirty look. "Shut up."

"Ok, I'll go to the left," she said. Then she dribbled to the basket with her left hand and scored.

She told me which way she was going and still scored on me! Diana is

Shooting for two against Diana and Lisa

extremely talented, but her confidence and her swagger set her apart from everyone else.

One of the greatest strengths of our program is that everyone who has ever played here is part of one big family. Every player who has come back to visit has been incredibly friendly and has fit right in with our current team. It's like they never left.

Photo courtesy of UConn Athletic Communications

THURSDAY, NOVEMBER 5, 2009

Today at the XL Center in Hartford, we played our second exhibition game. Our opponent was Southern Connecticut State University. We play about half our games at the XL Center, and the other half on campus at Gampel Pavilion. The reason we play in Hartford is because it allows more than 16,000 fans to attend our games, while there are only 10,167 seats in Gampel.

In the locker room before the game, Coach talked about some things we'll need if we want to be great. He said, "The first thing we need is some talent, which we have. The second thing we need is to have one or two guys step up and be leaders of our team. Everyone should know who these guys are when we step on the court. We need guys who compete in every single thing we do—guys who walk with their heads up and their shoulders back, and have so much confidence they will look you in your eyes and say, 'I'm gonna kick your *ss;' and then they do it. These guys make big plays when we need them; and they inspire the people around them to be better. I think we have a couple of these guys in our locker room, and we need them to show it on the court. All of our Championship teams have had a couple of these guys. They may not have been there initially, but they emerged as the season went on. If you're not one of these guys, get in line behind someone who is, and say, 'Let's go.'"

I really want to be the kind of leader Coach is looking for. I know I'm not vocal enough right now. I have always been a "nice guy," but nice only gets people so far. I know I can do this. I just need to step out of my shell and get it done. Nobody's perfect, but I usually do the right thing. Sometimes in the past, I would notice when my teammates were doing something wrong; but I just ignored it, rather than addressing it right there. Renee, on the other hand, addresses problems immediately and forcefully. This year I'm going to try to be more vocal when I need to be.

I played pretty well today. I was 4-4 from three-point range and finished with 17 points. Tina and Maya both played well, too, scoring 24 and 21, respectively. Maya is going to be incredibly good and really help us out. The game was terrible, though, because Southern Connecticut couldn't compete with us at any position. We annihilated them 119 to 58.

During a time-out toward the end of the game, Coach gave us two specific challenges. He said, "For the rest of the game, don't let them even attempt to shoot a three, and we're not gonna foul." The next play, they made a three, and then we fouled them on the following possession. Coach was furious. He doesn't care who we're playing, if we're up by a hundred and we do something stupid, we hear about it. He yelled at Tina during a time-out, saying a Division II kid was showing her up. She had just picked up her fourth foul with 10 minutes to go in the second half. He said, "I'm gonna keep you in, so you can foul out against Southern Connecticut State University. Not North Carolina, not Tennessee, but you're going to foul out against Southern Connecticut State University. That's embarrassing. I'm gonna keep you in there and let you embarrass yourself." Sure enough, two plays later, Tina set an illegal screen and fouled out against Southern Connecticut State University.

After the game, Coach pointed out that our big guys need to be better if we want to win a National Championship. He said, "How many of our big guys are great at something? I want you guys to name a big guy who is a great shooter." The room was silent.

"Who is a great defender?" Again, silence.

"Who is a great finisher around the basket?" Silence still.

"Who is a great rebounder?" A couple of people spoke up and said Brit was a great rebounder, and other guys were "pretty good" at certain things.

Coach said, "'Pretty good' isn't going to win a National Championship. Right now, we don't have enough big guys who aspire to be great."

Coach is always hard on our post players because they are not consistent enough. He's confident in what the guards will do each night, but he has to hope for results from the big guys. Coach is never satisfied with hoping. Until they show him what they can do every day, they will continue to hear about it.

TUESDAY, NOVEMBER 11, 2008

Tomorrow is our first official game. There's something special about the season opener. Although this is my fourth one, I'm just as excited as when I was a freshman. I'm a little more experienced now though. I've been following the same game day routine for three years. Every game day is the same. We go to classes in the morning and have shootaround in the afternoon. When we arrive at the gym, we watch film of the other team. This film shows us the opposing team's offensive sets, defenses, and player tendencies. Our coaches assemble a scouting report, which they pass out the day before. Scouting reports list the keys to the game, and the strengths and weaknesses of the team's personnel. During shootaround, we run through shooting drills and review our game plan. The coaches walk us through the other team's plays that we studied on film. Shootaround can be anywhere from a walk-through to a full practice, depending on Coach's mood. Today, we started at 1:30 and ended about 3:30, 30 minutes after schedule. Following shootaround, we have our pregame meal, which is always four hours before the game. We eat the same thing every time: chicken, pasta, baked potatoes, vegetables, soup, salad, and fruit.

An essential part of Connecticut Basketball is the traditions that make our program special. When Coach and CD came to UConn in 1985, they inherited a very weak program. It's amazing what they have built in the years since. Coach always ensures that his current players know about those who came before them and how big their contributions to our success have been.

Our program is so rich in tradition that some of it borders on superstition. First of all, we are *always* in the same order. We sit in the same seats when we watch film, on the plane, on the bus to and from games, and at our pregame meal. We start each drill with designated players, stretch in the same order, and stand in the same circle while Coach talks before practice.

Our pregame ritual is always the same. When we arrive at the gym, we watch a highlight tape of the previous game. This tape is always set to music, which is chosen by Kalana. This tradition has been passed down from Sue to Ashley Battle to Kalana. We stretch in the same order before warm-ups. Our warm-up is very precise and consists of the same drills before each game. CD hands me a small corner of a piece of paper that contains the starting times for film and the different parts of the warm-up. I always put the paper in my sock when she gives it to me, and remove it when we go to the locker room. However, once I forgot to take it out, and left it in my sock for the whole game. The blue ink bled onto my leg when I began to sweat. Since we won, I decided to keep it up. The piece of paper now remains in my sock for each game, and I always end up with a blue blob "tattooed" on my ankle. The timesheet responsibility was passed down to me from Ann, and was bestowed upon her by Maria.

We line up in order by height for the National Anthem. We each walk up the sideline and make a 90-degree turn onto the court like they do in the military. We all stand the same way with our hands behind our backs. During the pregame introductions, the starters sit in the same seats, and the non-starters stand in certain positions. Tonya massages my shoulders before the tip-off of every game. Renee wears a hair tie around her wrist for warm-ups, then she hands it to Tonya right before the game starts. The starters form a huddle, with each player in a particular order before the opening tip, and the non-starters do the same. During each time-out, the five players who are in the game sit on the bench, and everyone else huddles around Coach. The point guard must be in the middle of the five chairs, the two guards on inside seats, and the post players on the outside. Whichever point guard is out of the lineup has to kneel next to Coach so she knows what is going on when she enters the game. Jacquie always grabs the dry erase board and has it ready in case Coach needs it. Each time someone on our team makes a three-pointer, a player on the bench gives high fives to the rest of the subs. It's currently T's job. It was passed down to her through Marcy Czel and Stacey Marron.

Seniority is always respected in our program. The longer players have been in the program, and the more they've been through, the more respect they deserve. For each team meal, seniors walk to the front of the line, followed by the juniors, sophomores, and freshmen. The freshmen haven't proven anything, so they're at the bottom of the totem pole. They have to unload the bags off the bus, and they are responsible for stocking the locker-room fridge with Powerade and water. After games, they're required to be the last ones in the locker room to make sure everything is cleaned up.

All these things may seem silly at first, but we take great pride in our program's tradition. If I had the choice, I wouldn't want it any other way. I believe this type of order carries over to the court. If we are disciplined off the court, being disciplined on the court comes more naturally. I didn't understand this when I first got here, but I have since learned that every little thing we do is important. Now I can't stand to see one of my teammates with an un-tucked

A UConn tradition—
high fives after every three-pointer

shirt or wearing the wrong socks for a workout. We are all the same; we are a team. Each little deviation from the system takes away from that. It makes us special and different from every other team.

One of the best traditions in UConn Basketball is clapping during practice. Every player not actually involved in a drill is always clapping and cheering. This means we constantly encourage and applaud our teammates. We take pride in making our practices spirited and full of life. The habits we develop in practice become instinctive and carry over into games—both on the court and on the bench.

There's tradition, and then there's superstition. Many athletes do strange things for no good reason other than superstition. We have a few of those on

Encouragement from the bench

our team. Charde believes that if she makes her first shot during warm-ups, she will play poorly. Therefore, she misses her first jumper before every game. Tina listens to Jay-Z on the bus on the way to every game.

No one's superstitions were worse than Ashley Valley's. After our pregame meal, she always carried a plate with eight strawberries and four packets of sugar to her room. She ate them before she left for the game. Once, Ann stole a strawberry off Ashley's plate and ate it before she could say anything. We lost to Michigan State that night, and Ashley was convinced it was because she only had seven strawberries. She chewed three different pieces of gum each game—the first piece before warm-ups, the second five minutes prior to tip-off, and the third at halftime. She listened to a particular Mase song called "All I Ever Wanted" before each game. She wore the same bra and underwear for each game. She washed them (don't worry!)—but it's still weird!

CHAPTER 8

Gametime

WEDNESDAY, NOVEMBER 12, 2009

Today we played Stonybrook in our season opener. In his speech prior to the game, Coach said, "Every game, we should want to rip the other team's heart out from the start. Our goal should be to score 100 points every game for the entire season." We didn't quite get 100, but we were pretty close, scoring 98 to their 35.

After the game, the reporters asked what was different about this year. Coach said, "Well, we have more competitive guys."

"Who would that be?" they asked.

"I think our three most competitive players are Mel Thomas, Maya Moore, and Lorin Dixon. I don't think you will find three more competitive players. That's not to say the others aren't, but I am talking about being competitive in everything, whether it's sprinting or a drill. They want to win no matter what they're doing. I was telling Maya after shootaround, 'you didn't get double-figure rebounds in either of the two exhibition games, did you?' She told me she didn't. So then she came out tonight and got 10." Then Coach had to be the smart aleck he is and say, "I said the same thing to Tina, but about getting four rebounds."

Just like Coach said, Maya is always willing to step up to a challenge. It doesn't matter that she's a freshman and she usually doesn't know what she's doing. She still finds a way. The reporters asked Coach: "With the amount of talent that Maya has, why isn't she starting?"

"On all our best teams, freshmen never had to start because there were older guys ahead of them that had been around for a long time. There have been so many great players who didn't start their freshmen years—Diana Taurasi, Nykesha Sales, Shea Ralph, Mel Thomas, except when she was our starting point guard," he said with a laugh. "Maya might be the missing piece that we didn't have last year."

My freshman year, Coach was so desperate to find a point guard that he even put me in there. It was a pretty atrocious sight. I didn't even know where to go on the floor, and I was supposed to be the one directing the team. That experiment didn't last very long!

THURSDAY, NOVEMBER 15, 2007

Yesterday we played Holy Cross. Their coach is Bill Gibbons, who was one of my USA Basketball coaches last summer. He wrote me an e-mail a few weeks ago wishing me good luck this season, but said he wouldn't mind if I took a day off against his team. I didn't even need to score a point because Maya almost outscored them by herself. She came off the bench to score 31 points, while Holy Cross only scored 36 the entire game.

I thought we played pretty well in the first half, leading 47-20 at halftime. Then Coach stormed into the locker room, punching things and going absolutely insane. I sure wasn't expecting that. You would have thought we were down 30 points the way he was going crazy. His anger was directed 100 percent at Tina. "You don't do anything that good post players do! You have one rebound against Holy Cross. You don't rebound, you don't defend, and you don't run the floor. What do you do?" Tina gets the brunt of Coach's anger, but it's only because he's trying to make her better. She's a really good player, but she's not tough enough to be great...yet. The second he stops yelling at her is when she should be concerned. As long as he continues to expend his energy on her, she'll keep improving.

Right after the game, I had to go to the library to study. Thank God, we have a day off tomorrow!

SUNDAY, NOVEMBER 18, 2007

Tomorrow, we leave for the Virgin Islands to play in the Paradise Jam. Every few years, our program travels to some faraway place to play games over

Thanksgiving or Christmas break. Last Thanksgiving, we traveled to Italy to play exhibition games against two professional Italian teams.

Our "new team" first bonded on this trip to Italy. Each time a senior class leaves and a new group of freshmen come in, the team has to form a new identity. Teams often take on the personalities of their seniors. After they graduate, the remaining players have to figure out what their new roles will be. Ann, Barbara, Willnett, and Nicole's class had a very strong personality. They defined our team, and we followed their lead. The year after they graduated, we had no seniors. Ketia, Charde, Brittany, and I were juniors. We had to reinvent ourselves and organize a new team.

The culture in Italy was much different than in America. Obviously, their language and currency were different. Their electrical outlets were completely unlike ours, so we had to use converters for all our electric appliances. The majority of buildings were extremely old with extravagant detail. The food wasn't the same either. I learned the American imitation of Italian food tastes different from the real thing in Italy. Personally, I loved the food, but I can't say the same for all my teammates. There was a McDonald's in one of the cities we visited. Some of my teammates literally ran down the street because they couldn't get their Big Mac fast enough. Also, in the bathrooms, there is not only a toilet, but a bidet as well. Bidets look similar to toilets, but have a water faucet to cleanse the private areas after using the bathroom. We figured since we were there, we should experience *everything*, but that experience was pretty weird.

We aimed to see as many cities as possible while we were in Italy, so we spent hours upon hours driving up and down the country from Sorrento to Montella to Rome. The bus rides were long, so many of us slept to pass the time. On one trip, one of my teammates woke up suddenly with a full bladder. She walked to the bathroom at the back of the bus, only to find it locked. She asked the bus driver where she could go to the bathroom. He gave her an "I can't help you with that" look and said there was nowhere to stop for miles. She tried to hold it, but all of a sudden, the sound of liquid gushing onto the floor woke half the team. Everyone looked up to see her peeing in her pants. I have never laughed so hard in my entire life. (Sorry, I might get beaten up if I say her name!)

Charde, Kalana, me, and Tina at the Coliseum in Rome

Our first stop was Sorrento, where we visited Pompeii, a city that was destroyed in 79 AD by the volcanic eruption of Mount Vesuvius. The city was completely buried in ash and was lost for almost 1,700 years before its discovery in 1748. We visited Rome, where we saw St. Peter's Basilica, the Pope, and the Sistine Chapel.

The Sistine Chapel is famous for its beautiful ceiling, which was painted by Michelangelo over a period of seven years. The people of Rome are very adamant about protecting his artwork, so no one is permitted to take photographs. Also, no one is allowed to speak inside the Sistine Chapel because it is a holy place. They have guards that stand in the Chapel and repeat, "No photo, no video, shhhhh. No photo, no video, shhhhh." I heard it at least a hundred times over the 10 minutes I was in there. But apparently it didn't do much good because we decided we needed some memorabilia of our trip. We had one person on lookout for the guards, one blocking their view, and the other snapping a photograph. I should probably say a prayer for that one as well.

Every place we went was beautiful, but our most remarkable experience was in Coach's hometown, Montella, a place he had not been to since his childhood. There was a huge celebration to honor Coach's return, and he was treated like a hero. The people of Montella were so grateful that they presented Coach with his birth certificate and many of Montella's finest gifts in recognition of his achievements at UConn. Coach spoke to the large crowd in Italian, which was strange for us because we had never heard him speak it before. It was very touching to see Coach reunited with so many of his family members and an entire city honoring him.

Our last night in Italy, we played Cranium until four in the morning. Brit, T, and Megs were on the same team. T had to spell the word mozzarella backwards at a crucial point in the game. She said, "A-L-L-E-R..." Brit's eyes lit up with each letter; she was confident they would win. "A-Z-*T*..." Brit flipped out, "*T*! Everybody knows there's no *T* in mozzarella!" We were all laughing hysterically as T, Megs, and Brit were ready to kill each other. It was so intense that everyone was screaming about the game. Security came to our door with noise complaints at least three times before we finally had to shut the game down. After all that, no one even ended up winning the game.

This trip brought us closer together in many ways. Our chemistry was great, and we all knew we had a legitimate chance to win a National Championship. Sadly, our quest for that Championship fell short in the Regional Finals. We lost to LSU in the game we had to win to get to the Final Four. This year, Ketia, Charde, Brit, and I are seniors—a year older, wiser, and better prepared to lead our team. We're excited about the opportunity the Paradise Jam gives our team to build early momentum toward a championship season.

MONDAY, NOVEMBER 19, 2007

Today we arrived in the Virgin Islands. We left this morning at 5:30 from our apartment. Some of us tend to do things at the last minute, so we were all packing until about 2:30 in the morning. When we got on the bus this morning, one of our managers said, "Everybody double check and make sure you have your passports."

Renee turned around and said, "Do you have your passport?"

I started laughing, "Yes, Ne, I have my passport."

"Where's mine?"

"You're joking, right? How am I supposed to know where your passport is?"

For over a month, CD had been drilling us to make sure we knew where our passports were.

"Does Sarah have it? I think I might have given it to Sarah after we got back from Italy. Maybe Tonya has it." Sarah works in our office, and she keeps everyone organized. Renee ended up tracking it down before it was too late or else she might have been joining us in the Islands a few days later.

We had to fly commercial, which is very uncommon for us. Normally, we only go commercial for very long flights, like our trip to Italy. We charter almost every other flight during the season. Our bus driver pulls right up to our plane, where everyone passes through security and boards within five minutes. It's so much easier than waiting in the airport for hours. The entire plane is designed like the first class section on a commercial airline. We each have two big, leather seats to ourselves. We receive a full meal on the plane, and the flight attendants bring us about 10 different baskets full of chips, granola bars, cookies, and candy bars. We are spoiled because most teams have to fly commercial everywhere they go.

We wear matching UConn warm-up suits when we charter, but we have to dress up when we travel through regular airports. CD told us after practice yesterday to wear nice dress clothes because we were flying commercial. Megs gets a little confused sometimes and makes "blond" comments. Ketia had already left the gym and missed CD's instructions, so she asked Megs, "Why do we have to get dressed up tomorrow?"

"Oh, we're shooting a commercial right when we land in the Virgin Islands." Megs responded.

"Uh, are you sure about that Megs?" Ketia asked.

"Yea, CD said we had to dress up because of the commercial."

Brit cut in, laughing hysterically, "We are *flying* commercial, not shooting a commercial, you idiot!"

"Whoops! I knew I heard her say 'commercial'!"

When we got off the plane and walked outside, we rejoiced in the warm air. I am so excited to spend the whole a week on this gorgeous island. It was weird to see cars driving on the left side of the road. Signs are posted every few miles that read, "Remember: Drive on the other side!" A lot of tourists rent cars here, so I guess people forget sometimes.

After we got settled in our hotel, we drove across the island for dinner. This was an exciting trip in vehicles that were covered with tarps and had no doors. The restaurant, Oceana, was located on the beach, and we didn't leave for three and a half hours! Sometimes team dinners can be extremely long, so we have to find ways to entertain ourselves. Oceana, like many restaurants, placed fancy napkin designs on our table before we arrived. We asked the waiters to teach us how to fold them. Now I know how to make a swan, a rose, a water lily, and other standard designs.

Our bus ride to dinner in the Virgin Islands

TUESDAY, NOVEMBER 20, 2007

We had an early breakfast this morning, and then had practice in a high school gym where the temperature was close to 100 degrees. Everyone was dripping with sweat, so it was difficult to hold onto the ball. After practice, we were all dead tired, so we were anxious to get out of the heat and return to the hotel. Coach brought us into the usual huddle and told us we were lifting, and began passing out our lifting programs. We usually know which days are lifting days, but today it came as a surprise. We walked up five flights of stairs until we finally reached a tiny room with just a few weights. Part of being the best is doing what you don't want to do when you don't want to do it.

Coach told us, "It's not about where we are. We can't let the scenery distract us from what we came here to do." It's typically gorgeous weather, but it had been raining all day. Coach said sarcastically, "We didn't come here for sunshine anyway. We came here for rain and championships!"

CD had our hotel organize a scavenger hunt for us, so we could learn more about the island. My team was Maya, Renee, CD, and myself. I knew we'd win as soon as the names were called because everyone on our team has a cutthroat attitude. We walked down Main Street in search of answers to the clues we were given. We got a little too into it, running around in the rain like crazy people to be sure we'd win; and, of course, we did.

We went to a restaurant called the Old Stone Farmhouse for dinner. They served a three-course meal and dessert. We looked at the menu, astonished at how much food we would receive. Three courses! For my first course, I ordered lobster on French toast, followed by a knuckle sandwich, and chicken and dumplings. I tried to order something I understood because the menu was so complex it looked like a foreign language to me. The waiters walked around with a basket of bread, but would only place one tiny piece on our plates at a time. I was starving, and I wanted to just grab the whole basket. It would save them a lot of time if they just set the basket on the table, but apparently that's not what they do at nice restaurants. We hadn't eaten much all day, so we sat there like vultures, waiting for our first course to come out. Everyone got excited when we saw the plates come out. Then the waiter set one down, and everyone looked around, thinking, "What is this?" It was a mini pancake, about the size of a Ritz cracker, topped with a dot of sauce and a tiny piece of lobster. We could have eaten it all in one bite. Since that was the "appetizer" course, we all figured the next one would be bigger. The next two courses, however, were about the same size.

That's dinner?

Scavenger-hunters:
Maya, me, ChD, and Renee

Although we may not always get our food of choice, we appreciate the opportunities UConn has given us to eat at elegant restaurants. This has allowed us to try many foods we would otherwise never encounter. After we graduate, we'll probably never eat at restaurants like this again. Coach often says he expects the best from us every day at practice, and that's why we get the best in return.

WEDNESDAY, NOVEMBER 21, 2009

We practiced this morning in the gym where our games will be held during the tournament. We were free from noon until 6:15 to do whatever we chose, so a few of us walked to the beach. I brought one of my school books, which turned out to be pointless. It was impossible to read for more than 30 seconds at a time because I couldn't keep from looking at the view.

Cassie, on the other hand, was only concerned with tanning. On the way down to the beach, most of us stopped frequently to take pictures, but not Cassie. She sprinted all the way to the beach to get started on her tan. She flipped over a few minutes after the rest of us got settled, so I said "Oh, I guess it's time to flip."

"Oh yea. I'm on a timer," she said. She actually had an alarm set for every 15 minutes, so she'd be equally tanned on both sides! We left for a while to get in the hot tub, but she didn't want to miss any rays and wouldn't move from her spot.

When we left for dinner, Megs received an earful from CD for the length of her shorts. We're not allowed to wear anything too provocative because we're expected to represent the University of Connecticut positively. If someone is dressed inappropriately, CD takes our meal money. We went to Paradise Point, which is a resort at the top of the mountain. As the sky ride took us up the mountain, we could see the entire island. After dinner, we watched a show in which parrot-like birds rode tiny bikes and roller skates, and played basketball. After returning to our hotel, we all watched game film for 30 minutes.

When I got back to my room, I wrote a few pages for a marketing paper due at school, looked over my scouting report, and went to sleep.

Team photo at Paradise Point

THURSDAY, NOVEMBER 22, 2007

Today is Thanksgiving Day in America; but here on the island it's just an ordinary day. While others at home have been stuffing themselves with turkey and mashed potatoes, we have been practicing, watching film, and playing games. This is okay with me because there's nothing I would rather be doing. Both my Thomas family and my Connecticut family are here with me.

Tonight we played Stanford, the fifth-ranked team in the country. We started strong and built an early lead. We were up by nine at halftime, and ended up winning 66-54. We showed signs of greatness, but we're not there yet. We only know how to play at one pace, which is fast all the time. We need to learn when to push the ball, and when to slow it down and get a good possession.

Coach put Lorin in the game to guard All-American Candice Wiggins. Within five seconds, Lorin fouled her on the floor, so Stanford took the ball out-of-bounds on the side. The ball was inbounded to Candice, who shot a three-pointer in Lorin's face. The ball soared through the net and the ref blew his whistle, calling Lorin for her second foul. She stood in the corner with an attitude. We ran over to encourage her, "Get that look off your face. You're fine. Come on, let's go. You'll get it back." But Lorin didn't budge. Instead she pouted in the corner longer than she had even been in the game. That's all Coach had to see to send someone to the scorer's table to replace her. Coach isn't the type to take a player out of the game after one mistake, but if a player has an attitude or doesn't hustle, he'll yank her out of the game as fast as he can throw a sub off the bench. Lorin didn't see the floor again after that. Maybe that will teach her not to pout again.

After the game, CD told Renee and me that we needed to talk to Charde about the way she has been acting lately. Being a captain is harder than it may sound. Not only do we have to worry about ourselves and our playing abilities, but also we have to make sure that everything else is going smoothly. Lately, Charde has seemed removed from everything we're doing. It seems like something is bothering her, or she just doesn't care. We're not really sure. Renee and I decided to go to her room after the game to try and determine what her problem was. As we walked into her room, I said, "Hey, Char Char. We'd like to talk with you."

"Okay," she replied.

"It seems like something's been bothering you lately, and we want to help."

"I'm fine."

"We want to see you do well. We want to see you succeed. You're a big part of this team, and we just want to make sure we're all on the same page." Her response was a blank stare.

"Do you want to talk about anything? We're here for you if you do." Again, nothing.

"Char, you seem so distant, so removed from everything we're trying to do. We need you to be a part of it. Are you sure nothing's wrong?" Her eyes stared back at mine. No response.

"Char, I'm asking you a question. Can I get some type of response, please?" Nothing.

"I would rather you tell me to get the hell out of your room than look at me like you don't care about what I have to say. Can you just talk to me?" Nothing.

"Do you even care about our team?" By this point, I felt like I was talking to a wall.

I went into her room with the intention of trying to help, but by the end I was so mad I could barely talk. This was my senior year, and I wasn't going to let her mess it up.

"You don't give a damn about our team. You may not care about what we're trying to do here, but we do. That's so messed up." She just sat there and stared at me. I wanted to punch her. I yelled at her some more and stormed out of the room. "Well, that went well," I said sarcastically to Renee.

We never figured out what was wrong with her. Charde's always kept everything inside her. She never tells me anything when I ask how she's feeling or if she's having a problem. Was she depressed? Was something wrong at home? Was she just a jerk who didn't care about our team? I guess I'll never know. I really wish I could have gotten her to open up; but instead, the mystery continues.

SATURDAY, NOVEMBER 24, 2007

Yesterday, we beat Old Dominion 86-43 which earned us a spot in the championship game against Duke tomorrow. Today we had free time in the morning, so our coaches scheduled a catamaran trip for our team. The captain anchored the ship off the coast of Shipwreck Island, so we could all go snorkeling. Everyone looked funny in their masks, snorkels, and flippers. The island was called Shipwreck Island because many years ago, a boat crashed into the rocks and sunk. We all had fun exploring the wreckage. Since the fish stay close to the rocks, we swam mostly near the shore to see them. The number, variety, and bright colors of the reef fish were amazing.

We brought an underwater camera, so Megs decided to take pictures of Jacquie and me with the fish. Jacquie and I posed underwater near the rocks. When we surfaced, Jacquie was holding her arm and screaming, "Something bit me! Something bit me!"

I saw her brush her arm against the coral on her way up, so I told her, "Jac, I think you just scraped it against the coral and it's probably just burning from the salt water."

"No, something bit me! I felt it!" She was close to tears. "You guys, it really hurts." The three of us had a long swim back to the boat. Poor Jacquie, she was holding her injured arm with her good one, so she had to swim with just her flippers!

When we finally made it back to the boat, she showed her arm to the captain. By then, she had a puffy, red rash from her wrist all the way up to her

Jac and I check out the coral near Shipwreck Island

shoulder. The captain told her she had fire coral, which is the poison ivy of the sea. He gave her a bag of ice to ease the pain. Our trainer wrapped her arm from her fingers all the way to her shoulder. She wasn't able to practice that day. Not only was she in pain, but the rash was contagious as well. The catamaran trip was a fun adventure for most of us, but not for Jac!

Tonight, Ketia's dad threw a surprise birthday party for her mom. This was at the house they had rented for the trip. All the players and parents gathered for the celebration. Our families are a very closely knit group. Before each home game, the parents who are in town join together for a pregame meal at various restaurants—just like us. After every game, we hug and socialize with every one of our teammate's family members. Once players join our program, they instantly inherit 13 sets of adopted parents.

On the way back from the party, our whole team sang a remix to the nursery rhyme "Baa Baa Black Sheep." It was unlike anything I've ever heard. Our performance was videotaped, which is pretty scary because it will be documented forever! One of our local news stations in Connecticut gives us a video camera to catch "Behind the Scenes" footage on big trips. Last year for the NCAA Tournament, T and I choreographed a synchronized swimming routine for the camera. The conclusion of the routine was to perform handstands underneath the water, with a matching leg split. On our last take, we executed the move to perfection and our legs came together at exactly the same time. This was completely by chance because we had no clue what we were doing. That might have been my proudest moment from the tournament last year!

SUNDAY, NOVEMBER 25, 2007

Today we played Duke, the eighth-ranked team in the country. We won the Paradise Jam title 74-48. After receiving our trophy, and the traditional championship hats, we celebrated on the court and had a blast. Hopefully, this was the first of many championships. We felt really good about beating a top-10 team by 26 points.

I truly believe we are the best team in the country, and there's nothing anyone can do to stop us. We have so much depth, so many threats, and a lot of experience. Each one of us has made sacrifices to be here. Most of us could have gone to another school and averaged 20 points a game, but instead we chose to come to Connecticut where we play every day with 10 other High School All-Americans. We all contribute our individual strengths, and together that makes us a great team. Each one of our five starters averaged double figures last year. It's exciting that we're all back together—a year older and stronger. I feel the same way I did when I was a senior in high school. My mentality then was that my team was unstoppable. Losing was not even a thought in the back of my mind. My confidence was justified as we went undefeated and won our State Championship. I think my team can win every game again this year.

Since we have to leave early tomorrow and wouldn't get much sleep anyway, we decided to go out to the beach at about 3:00 in the morning. Kaili is friends with a few of the Stanford girls, so she invited them to come with us. Because it was so late, we were the only people on the beach. Our team built a sandcastle shaped like Gampel. We played games and just enjoyed the relaxing atmosphere, forgetting about basketball for a couple of minutes.

Gampel Pavilion construction crew

Those minutes soon passed, however, and we began talking with the Stanford girls about the differences in our programs. We compared preseason workouts and practice. One of the girls told us their coach made them watch our warm-up. She aspired to get her program to the highest level, so she wanted her team to learn from us. It was weird they told us this after we had beaten them. I'm not surprised, though, that other coaches want to emulate some of Coach's routines and strategies. After all, he has won five National Championships.

MONDAY, NOVEMBER 26, 2009

Today, our trip back from the Virgin Islands didn't go too smoothly. When we arrived at the airport at 6:00 in the morning, it took forever for all of us to check in. When I reached the counter, I was told they didn't have my reservation. A couple of my teammate's reservations didn't appear either. Eventually we discovered that one of our travel agents made a mistake, stranding six of us in the airport for another eight hours. We tried to entertain ourselves, but once we ran out of fun, we turned to sleep. I bought a pillow from the gift shop and slept for hours, sprawled over three seats. We finally got a flight to JFK in New York City. The van we took back to school had a huge television screen, so we watched movies all the way home. We finally made it, though it was hardly the trip we expected.

WEDNESDAY, DECEMBER 5, 2009

Today we played Virginia and I needed five points to reach my 1,000th point. There was so much hype from the media leading up to the game that I wish they had never told me. I just wanted to hit a couple of shots early on and get it over with. That's probably why I missed my first four shots, and it took me 23 minutes to score two baskets! Coach drew up a couple of plays for me, but I just couldn't get the ball in the net. At one point, Brit asked me, "Mel, how many points do you need?"

"I need five!" I responded.

"Get your five, then!" she said. I finally made a three at the end of the first half to get within two. Every time I touched the ball after that, the crowd went crazy. In the second half, Kalana drove to the hoop and kicked it out to me around the free-throw line and I finally knocked in my 1,000th point. Kalana proceeded to tell me the only reason I scored 1,000 points was because of her assist. It was never a goal of mine, but I appreciate it's a huge achievement. I became only the 29th player in UConn history to join the 1,000 Point Club. It was more important, though, that we won 75-45. This improved our record to 7-0.

CHAPTER 9

Nothing is Guaranteed

I'll remember last night for the rest of my life. We played South Carolina at Gampel, our first game in over a week. We started off a little shaky, but ended up playing pretty well. The play that sticks in my mind happened at the end of the first half. On a fast break play, Kalana drove at full speed from the right sideline to the basket. She was airborne for an easy lay up when a defender ran into her—knocking her off balance. When she landed, her body was in an awkward position and her right leg collapsed. She fell to the ground, and immediately grabbed her leg yelling, "It's my knee! It's my knee!" She tried to stand up, but couldn't bear any weight on it, so our athletic trainer, Rosemary Ragle (Rosie), helped her off the floor and into the training room. Our perfect season flashed before my eyes. Kalana is one of the strongest and most athletic players on our team. She wasn't supposed to get hurt. That wasn't part of our plan. I tried to be optimistic, but it didn't look good.

Coach left the court and was gone for most of the second half checking on Kalana, which was very unusual. I have never before seen him leave the court to be with an injured player, so we all knew it was bad. He usually leaves that responsibility with Rosie. At halftime, we were ahead 43-19, so no one was thinking about the game. We were much more concerned about our fallen teammate. Our mood in the locker room was pretty somber because no one knew for sure what was wrong with Kalana.

In the second half, not having either Kalana or Coach on the court was very strange. We tried to play through it, but horrible thoughts were in the

Kalana being helped off court after her ACL injury

back of our minds. When we got to the locker room after the game, we all heard the news. It was what everyone hoped it wasn't—a torn ACL.

When Coach came into the locker room, we could tell he was shaken up. He paced back and forth for a few minutes, without saying a word. It seemed as though he was trying to postpone addressing the situation. When he finally spoke, he said:

"It's so strange the way things repeat themselves. Nine years ago,

December 14, it was just an ordinary day at practice, and we were doing 11-man break. Sue had the ball and she pulled up for a short jumper. She fell down, but got up right away. I asked what happened and she said 'I don't know, that just felt kinda funny.' Turned out, she had a torn ACL and here we are nine years later on December 17, almost the exact same day, and Kalana does the same thing.

"Everything happens for a reason. We don't know what that reason is right now, but maybe it's to remind us that nothing is guaranteed. It's like the saying, 'Yesterday is history, tomorrow is a mystery.' Tomorrow for Kalana is not going to come for six to eight months. You guys think you have forever to play basketball because that's what you've always done, and that is what you feel like you're always gonna do. When you're a freshman, you feel like you have forever at Connecticut; but then, all of a sudden, you're a senior. You look around and your basketball career only lasts three more months here."

He couldn't be more right. I can't believe this is it for me. This has been my dream since I was a little kid, and I'm going to work as hard as I can these last three months to assure I leave here with a National Championship.

I feel so terrible for Kalana. I can't believe this really happened. I can't even imagine how she's feeling right now. Everyone went to her apartment after the game to see how she was doing. She pretended to be in good spirits, but in truth, she was devastated. That was the first time I ever remember seeing Kalana cry.

Everything I had been thinking about leading up to the game didn't seem important anymore. Watching someone you love be devastated by a seemingly random event adds new perspectives to your own life. First, it makes you appreciate the opportunities you still have; and second, it forces you to focus on what is most important in your life. I was upset that I wasn't playing too well, but that just seems stupid now. At least I have the opportunity to play another day, another game.

WEDNESDAY, DECEMBER 19, 2009

We arrived here in San Diego yesterday. Before we left, I had to say goodbye to my boyfriend, Tyvon Branch (TyTy), because he's leaving to train for the NFL Combine. He played football for Connecticut. He was a senior this year, but graduated early so he could train in California for the next two months. He's been my biggest supporter and my best friend for four years, so it sucks that he's leaving. He's the one who keeps me sane when basketball is rough and I'm stressed out from school.

It's really strange not having Kalana at practice. Every day, each player lines up in the exact same order for our drills because it helps us move more quickly from one drill to the next. There are certain drills that Kalana always started. Today, we ran our fast break, which is a drill where four players run up and down the court four times to score as quickly as possible. Renee, Kalana, Charde, and I always started the drill. We took off today, and we didn't notice until we were halfway down the court that we only had three people! That was the first time it sunk in that she really wasn't on the court with us. Renee and I should have addressed the situation before practice and decided who would replace Kalana in the drills. But I don't think we were ready to face it yet. I don't think our team was ready either.

On the other hand, life goes on, our season goes on, and we're going to have to find a way to win without her. It was evident through our whole practice how big a presence Kalana has been on the court and how vital she's been to our team. After practice, Coach said, "We have a big void in our system, and so far, no one has stepped up to fill it." He challenged Meg, Lorin, or T to raise their games enough to replace what we're missing without Kalana. Coach always challenges our big guys to step up because he never thinks they are reaching their full potential. He said his daughter, Alysa, who doesn't play basketball and was home in Connecticut, has a better chance of filling that void than a few of our post players. It will be interesting to see who rises to the challenge.

THURSDAY, DECEMBER 20, 2007

Yesterday, the first 30 minutes of practice were non-stop running. Coach wouldn't let us stop because he didn't think every person was sprinting through every drill. He said, "I'm glad I left my family during the holidays, so I could come here and watch this bull." You can always count on him to be completely sarcastic.

Coach had us do shell drill, which is four-on-four and focuses on defense.

Maya was on the blue team, which continually plays defense. She jumped in the air at a shot fake, and her player drove past her to the basket. Coach always stresses never to leave our feet because once we do, we're beat. Coach said, "Maya, you owe me a suicide after practice, and anyone else who leaves their feet the rest of practice does too." A suicide is a drill in which players start at the end line, sprint to the free-throw line and back, then to half-court and back, then to the far free-throw line and back, and finally to the far end line and back. Tina was standing on the sideline, not even in the drill at this point. She raised her hand. Coach looked at her with an annoyed look on his face "What!"

She said, "I jumped."

He stared at her, completely confused, and said, "Okay, you can give me one too if you want to."

I looked at Megs and whispered, "Did she just tell on herself?"

Megs started laughing, "Yea! She's so stupid! Who does that?"

She must have been confused or misheard what Coach asked because, trust me, Tina would not be the one to volunteer herself to run anywhere.

Our Director of Basketball Operations, Jack Eisenmann, takes care of many organizational details on road trips. There have been times in the past where people have tried to sneak in and videotape our practices and shootarounds, so he looks out for that as well. During practice, Jack saw a silhouette in the stands in the very last row. He walked up all the stairs in the huge arena to check out the situation, only to discover that the man was actually a cardboard cutout. We all laughed about it and thanked Jack for protecting us from the cardboard man.

FRIDAY, DECEMBER 21, 2007

When we travel, we often get to experience something interesting in each city. Tomorrow, we are going to the San Diego Zoo. Today, our team had the opportunity to visit a U.S. Naval Base and tour the U.S.S. Ronald Reagan. This is one of the top aircraft carriers in the world, and is home to 6,000 sailors. Two guys who played basketball at the U.S. Naval Academy gave us a tour. One said, "Everyday, we woke up around 5:30, went to class, went to practice, trained for the Navy, and then went to sleep early enough so we could do it all

Touring the U.S.S. Reagan

again the next day. So when you think you have it bad, think again." I have so much respect for all they do. I feel like I have a full plate, so I can only imagine how much they do every day.

Coach turns everything we do into a learning experience. There is a lot more to playing basketball for UConn than just the Xs and Os. Coach teaches us a lesson whenever he sees the opportunity. He asked the Captain, "If any of your men messes up a landing and blows up a 35-million-dollar plane, do you give them another chance?"

The captain replied, "Well, we might give them a second chance, but never a third."

Coach said, "Well, I'll keep that in mind the next time these knuckleheads are begging for a third and fourth chance to get something right."

He relates everything to what he tries to teach us each day. The captains expect perfection from their pilots, just like Coach demands it from us.

He tells us, "You have to expect perfection. You'll never reach it, but the more you expect, the closer you'll get." Everything we do has to be as close to perfect as possible. Every cut has to be precise. Every pass has to be crisp. Every line must be touched. Drills are started over if we fumble a pass or miss a layup.

Each year for Christmas, Coach gives us an inspirational book to read. One was about the military because he often compares us to soldiers. Coach says, "If you ask a soldier why he is fighting, he will say he fights for everything America stands for—our freedoms and our rights. But what he really fights for are the men who are sitting to the left and right of him. We carry that over to the court by playing together. If one of you guys gets knocked down, you know that four other players will be there to pick you up. If you don't feel responsible for your teammates today at practice, what's going to happen to them? Today? Absolutely nothing. If you're in the Marines and you don't take responsibility for your friends, what's going to happen to them? They're gonna get blown up. Here, if you don't fight together as a team today, you are all going to get blown up in March when it really matters. What is equivalent to getting blown up in basketball? Losing in the tournament and sending your seniors home empty handed."

The entire experience of visiting the U.S.S. Ronald Reagan was truly extraordinary. We think what we are doing is hard, but it's nothing compared to what is being done by the people who put their lives on the line every day for our country.

After the carrier tour, we went back to the hotel for our pregame meal. We then played San Diego State and won 85-53. Maya started tonight for Kalana, who couldn't even travel with us because she had surgery this morning. The MRI results showed that not only did she tear her ACL, but also her meniscus and LCL. I can only imagine how scared she must be. I feel awful that she has to go through this without us there to help her. In addition, she has to spend Christmas in Connecticut, laid up in bed.

SATURDAY, DECEMBER 22, 2009

I took six classes during fall semester, so I wouldn't have to carry a full load in the spring. If student-athletes plan their schedules correctly, many have to take only one class in their final semester. I was late declaring my major, so I couldn't begin taking classes in the School of Business until the spring of my junior year. This left me with only three semesters to complete the required courses for a Business degree. This semester, I had a tremendous amount of work with my six classes. With such a heavy load, I had to spend more time studying than ever before.

After each semester ends, our professors post their students' grades online. As of yesterday, I had received five grades—all As. I was waiting on only one grade, so I was positive I had a perfect 4.0. Today I checked online to get my last grade. Indeed, it was an A, but it was followed by an ugly little dash that transformed it to an A minus. I couldn't believe my eyes. I wiped my finger over the mark to make sure it wasn't something stuck on the computer screen. But it was an actual line—a tiny line that spoiled my 4.0. The class was a one-credit course, so my GPA came out to be a 3.97. I e-mailed my teacher to ask if I could turn in an extra credit assignment or rewrite a draft. I doubt it will work, but I figured it was worth a try. That stupid little dash ruined my day!

WEDNESDAY, DECEMBER 26, 2009

Although I would never pass up an opportunity to see my family and friends, I would almost rather not go on breaks because the coaches think they need to "get us back in shape" when we return. We practiced for over three hours today, which was mostly non-stop running. T and Charde were late because their flights were delayed, so we only had one sub when we scrimmaged. I'm not sure why, but the bottom of my feet started hurting toward the end of practice and I could barely run. It might be because I was wearing new shoes, but after practice I looked at my feet and nothing seemed to be wrong with them at all.

THURSDAY, DECEMBER 29, 2009

Today at practice, I could barely move because my feet were hurting again. I had no idea what was wrong, but the bottoms of my feet burned. Coach was trying to kill us to make up for the fact that Kalana was hurt. He told us after practice, "I know it's been a death camp the past couple days, but we work harder than every other team in the country, and it's all going to pay off." He came up to me after practice and said, "What's wrong with you? You look like you're hurt." I told him I was fine. But there was something wrong with me. After practice when I took off my shoes, I noticed that huge blisters had formed in the same place on both my feet. Almost the whole pad of my fore-foot was one big blister. Rosie had to cut them open and fill them with zinc oxide to help them heal. I felt like a big baby because I could barely run, and it was only blisters. At least it wasn't anything worse; they'd be gone in a few days.

There's a thin line between playing through pain and being stupid. After the strenuous workouts we go through every day, it's inevitable that some part of our bodies will hurt. There's a big difference between hurting and being injured. It's hard to judge when to suck it up and when to speak up. If I had approached Rosie about my feet right away, my whole problem could have been avoided.

SATURDAY, DECEMBER 29, 2007

We played Hartford today, and I didn't play well. I felt like I missed every shot I took. It wasn't even a competitive game as they only scored 24 points; but it was still frustrating. I'm trying to stay positive and confident. One thing I've learned over the years is that one game doesn't define a player. Every failure is an opportunity to come back better and stronger. I use every bad performance as motivation to work harder. I'm still doing what I love, and I have many more chances to show what I can do.

SUNDAY, DECEMBER 30, 2007

After practice today, we had our annual Secret Santa exchange. We picked names out of a hat and give presents to the person whose name we drew. It's always fun to try to guess who picked your name. It's supposed to be a surprise, but usually half the people know who their Secret Santa is by the time we exchange gifts. Coach picked my name. When he walked toward me with the box, I had no idea what to expect. I didn't have much trust in Coach's fashion sense. He certainly knows how to take care of himself as he always looks stylish in his Armani suits. I was doubtful, however, that choosing a present for a 22-year-old girl was really his thing.

The first gift I opened was tiny doll clothing. I looked at him, completely confused, wondering why he would possibly buy that for me. Coach isn't one to keep his opinions to himself.

"I thought this shirt looked about the same size as the one you had on last week." He always teases me that everything I wear is too small. When I opened my second present, I found lotion and perfume which I was pretty impressed with. Coach said, "When I was walking around the mall looking for your present, I passed a girl who smelled like you. I stopped her and asked what she was wearing. She told me; so I bought it." I didn't think this was a normal way to buy a present, but it's Coach. What can you expect?

TUESDAY, JANUARY 1, 2008

Happy New Year! Last night, we went to Coach's New Year's party. I think we're invited each year, just to keep us out of trouble. But we always have a great time. Life has a funny way of turning itself around. Only two days ago, I was so frustrated with basketball it was making me crazy. I have been shooting the ball poorly lately, and I know I'm a lot better than that. When I can't do the one thing that's expected of me, I feel worthless. In the past, I've spent hours upon hours trying to figure out what's wrong with my shot. Over the years, I've learned that stressing about it only makes it worse. Shooting is about 90 percent mental. If players don't have their confidence and mindset right, there's no way they can be successful. Sometimes, if I just step away and relax, I come back a whole lot better. That's what I did, and now I'm happy as can be. I played really well in our game against Army, scoring 19 points.

FRIDAY, JANUARY 4, 2008

Yesterday we played at Villanova, which was our first Big East game. Every game in the conference is important because one loss can cost us the league title. Teams have to prove they're the best over a span of 16 games. We definitely proved it tonight with an 88-38 win.

When we played at Villanova my sophomore year, Ketia saw a sign that said "The Pavilion" on their arena. She said, "Oh, it's a pav-a-lion, just like Gampel!"

We all laughed hysterically, "What did you say Keesh?"

"A pav-a-lion, like Gampel."

"You mean pavilion (pa-vil-yen)?"

She had been playing in Gampel Pavilion for two years, and still didn't know how to pronounce the word! Of course, we had to tease her a little bit since we were back there again.

SUNDAY, JANUARY 13, 2008

Last night we played Louisville on their home court. It was the first real test we have had in a long time. We've been beating teams by so much that to have a tough game was kind of unexpected. We were all feeling pretty invincible, so it was good for us to be challenged. We won 92-71, which is still a large margin, but we've been beating teams by 50 points!

Louisville is only an hour and a half from my house, so many of my friends and family members were able to make the trip. My mom has nine brothers and sisters, so they wore matching t-shirts and made up their own cheering section. My high school principal and teachers came, and also some of my old teammates. They have been incredibly supportive of my UConn career. I've been blessed to have many great people in my life. It meant a lot to me to have some of them there. My principal ordered our game package online, so my teachers can watch all my games on the projector at my high school. Connecticut Public Television (CPTV) broadcasts all of our games that are not shown on a national network. This gives Husky fans all over the world the opportunity to watch our games live on television or on streaming video.

We stayed overnight in Louisville after the game because today is Sunday, and we don't have to hurry home for classes. We practiced in Cardinal Arena this morning, and the entire Louisville team was there to watch. The situation felt a little awkward to us; and the Louisville players seemed uncomfortable with it as well. They looked like they didn't want to be there. The Louisville coach asked if his team could observe our practice. He's a new coach who is trying to build his program, so he looked to Coach for guidance. This was an unusual request, but Coach agreed. He is confident that we can still beat a team after letting them watch everything we do.

MONDAY, JANUARY 14, 2008

Today we arrived in Syracuse. The plane ride from Hartford to Syracuse was only 20 minutes. We practiced in Manley Fieldhouse, which is Syracuse's old gym. Tomorrow, we'll play in the Carrier Dome, which is a 50,000 seat football stadium. The court is on one end while the rest of the field is blocked off, but still visible. It's unlike anywhere else I've ever played. The listed capacity for basketball games is 33,000, but Syracuse Women's Basketball averages less than 2,000 fans for their home games. It's weird to play in front of so many empty bleachers. I'm sure it would be a fun place to play if the arena was sold out.

My boyfriend is from Syracuse. He's still training in California, but 17 of his family members are coming to the game. He has a huge family, and I'm really excited they get to watch us play. I know at least 17 people in the stands will be rooting for UConn!

CHAPTER 10
Twist of Fate

TUESDAY, JANUARY 15, 2008

It's 3:37 in the morning. I'm lying in my bed crying and I can't fall asleep. I have called TyTy so many times that I feel bad calling him again. I just don't feel like this is real. Why the hell did this happen to me? I can't believe that I'll never again put on a UConn jersey. When I took it off today in the locker room, I completely lost my composure, knowing that my career was over. I never thought that all the sprints, the tears, the emotion, and the sacrifices would end like this. It doesn't make any sense. I used to believe that everything really does happen for a reason. Now I'd like to know what the reason for this is.

It happened with two minutes left in the game. I drove toward the baseline, stopped and pivoted to the right to pass the ball behind me. My right knee turned to the inside as I fell backwards and landed on my butt. I screamed and grabbed my knee. I lay on the floor for a few seconds, then got up and tried to run, but I just couldn't. Everything happened incredibly fast, so it was all a blur. Initially, it was painful, but I was more shocked than anything. I was thinking, "Uh oh. It's my knee." I have never had any problems with my knees before, so I was scared to death. Still, I didn't think it was anything serious; I just thought I tweaked it a little. Rosie came out on the court, but I hobbled right past her to the bench. I hate when players lie on the floor, and then, when they finally get back up, they're completely fine. Most of the time, players can get off the court on their own.

The worst part was that when I fell, I dropped the ball; and a Syracuse player took it all the way down the court for a bucket and a foul to cut our

My biggest nightmare

lead to three. When Renee saw me go down, all she could do was stare in shock while they dribbled right past her down the court. The game was already terrible, and there was no way it should have been that close. Coach benched all of the post players midway through the first half, so we had five guards on the floor the majority of the game. Even I was playing in the post for a while, which was not a good situation. It was by far the worst game we played all year. For me to go down in a game like that was awful.

As soon as my butt hit the bench, Rosie told me to go to the locker room. I limped back to the locker room with so many thoughts running through my mind. First of all, we were only up three when I left the game. I was freaking out. It was down to the wire with Syracuse and I couldn't help my teammates or even see what was going on. Secondly, it began to sink in that my knee

128

Photo courtesy of *Hartford Courant* / Kevin Rivoli

might really be hurt. When I think of knee injuries, I just assume they're bad, but I was trying to figure out how serious this was. When I first got to the locker room, I walked back and forth, thinking in my head, "I wonder if I can go back in." I tried to run a couple of steps to test my knee. I was running with an ugly limp, but I almost convinced myself it wasn't that bad.

Rosie asked me how it felt. "It doesn't really hurt. It just feels weird. It feels a little off, like something's not exactly normal." At this point, I wasn't thinking that I tore anything. I didn't think it hurt enough. I could walk, not well, but nonetheless I could walk. Rosie had me climb onto the table so she could examine my knee. The look on her face wasn't reassuring. I'm not sure at exactly what point I realized it was bad, but my tears began to flow. I screamed the F-word at the top of my lungs. Then I heard the crowd going crazy and I started thinking about the game. I sat up, "Rosie, what do you think the score is?"

"Now you just need to lie down and let me look at your knee, okay?" I relaxed for a couple of seconds and then I started sobbing again, wondering if my college career was over. Then the crowd roared again.

"Rosie, how much time do you think is left?" Then a couple more F-bombs came screaming out of my mouth.

She said, "I just need you to calm down so I can look at your knee." She tugged on it again.

"Rosie, what do you think it is—honestly? Is it bad?"

"Honestly, I think it's your ACL, but you're not really letting me get a good examination."

I started sobbing again. I'm not exactly sure why the F-word kept coming out every five seconds, but I couldn't help it. I heard the crowd roar again, and all of a sudden I jumped off the table and said, "Rosie I'm goin' back out there."

"Are you sure you want to?" I couldn't take it anymore. The crowd was going crazy. I had no idea what was going on, so I had to get out there.

"Do you wanna wipe your face?"

"Rosie, that's really the least of my worries right now." I'm sure I looked like hell with tears and mascara streaming down my face, but I really didn't care.

If I had been in any kind of normal state, I probably would have looked in the mirror and screamed; but at that moment, it wasn't important to me at all. I limped back out to the court and sat down on the floor at the end of the bench. I sat in front of Vinny, and he grabbed my hand because I was such an emotional wreck. We were ahead by four with less than a minute left, but I was so nervous I could barely watch. We pulled it out, winning by six points 65-59. When I walked through the line to shake hands, I was in complete shock. I didn't know what to think. As I limped off the court, all our fans were incredibly supportive and were assuring me I'd be fine. One of the media guys came chasing after me, asking what was wrong with me. I'm sure it wasn't because he was concerned. He just wanted a good story.

When we returned to the locker room, Rosie tugged on me a little more, and then took me to the training room to see the Syracuse doctor. After he finished his exam, he asked, "Do you mind if my students examine you?"

I wanted to say, "Do you mind if I kick you in the face?" Instead, though, I replied, "Sure, go ahead," with a forced smile. Three more people started tugging on my knee, asking the exact same questions. The consensus was that it appeared my ACL was torn. They gave me a pair of crutches and I left the exam room, not knowing what to do or where to go.

I made my way back to the locker room, but the mood was so hostile that I wanted to leave immediately. I wonder what Coach said to them because it was like somebody had died in there. I don't know if it was because of our performance or their concern for my injury, but it was not a place I wanted to be. The looks on my teammates' faces were probably worse than the look on my own. I left the locker room with no destination and crutched aimlessly down the hallway. I walked out to the court, wondering if TyTy's family had stuck around after the game. If I'd had a phone, finding them would have been a whole lot easier. Kaili came down the hall and saw me looking lost. She asked, "Where are you going?"

I looked around, searching for an answer. "I don't know," I said helplessly. Tears began to roll down my face. Kaili wrapped her arms around me and comforted me as I lay on her chest like a little baby. I wiped my eyes, and hopped back to the locker room.

After the game, I wanted to call my mom but my phone was in a box on the bus. For all the games, the coaches make us leave our phones behind, so they aren't a distraction.

Coach approached me in the locker room and handed me his phone. I said, "Who am I supposed to call?"

"Whoever you want. I heard you needed a phone."

That was all he said to me that night. I think he was badly shaken up from the game, and saw our perfect season slipping away one ACL at a time. Still, I was upset. I had given my heart and soul to his program for four years, and now it's over with a torn knee, and he had nothing to say to me. I called my house, my mom, and my dad, but no one answered. Everyone on my team was in an awful mood because we almost lost to Syracuse. It was the worst situation ever. I was all alone with a torn ACL, feeling absolutely miserable.

My mom, who is my biggest supporter, has been to almost every game I've played since I was 10 years old. But on this night, her boss had given her tickets to a play, so she went to the show and taped my game to watch later. Her friend Devon, who was watching the game, texted her and asked, "Is Mel okay?" My mom freaked out and immediately left the play because she always worries about everything. She calls me all the time and frantically asks, "Mel, are you okay? I just had this really bad feeling that something was wrong with you!" I always tell her that I'm fine, and start laughing, because her mother's intuition is *never* right. The one time something actually was wrong with me, she had no idea!

I finally talked to my family when I got on the bus. Of course, my mom was crying hysterically. She tried to act like she wasn't, but she didn't cover it up too well. She told me she was catching a flight the next morning to come and be with me, which was comforting.

Megs, Cassie, Jacquie, and I always use the same bottle of hairspray before each game, and I have been the supplier of it the past two seasons. On the bus, I handed it to Jacquie and said, "Jac, I'm passing this down to you." Ann Strother passed it to me, and now I was passing it on to Jac.

She said, "No, I don't want you to! It might not even be that bad."

"Yes, it is that bad. This is a huge responsibility. Are you sure you're ready for it?" I told her jokingly.

Then I said to Kalana, "Well at least you have a friend now."

"I don't want a friend!" she replied.

Everybody told me to stop talking like that because I might be fine. But I knew my knee wasn't right. And I knew I wasn't okay. I kept joking around because that was the only thing I could do to keep from crying. The 20-minute plane ride seemed much longer on the way home. On the bus from the airport to campus, I called my friend Chrissy Monaco. She came to UConn with hopes of making our team as a walk-on her freshman year. Instead, she broke her foot and couldn't play. She lived with Ketia, Charde, and me our first year, and we've been great friends ever since. She's been there for me through everything, so she told me she'd be right over when we got back at 2:00 in the morning.

I was still all sweaty and smelly from the game, so I needed to shower. By this point, I couldn't bend or apply pressure to my knee. Brit and Chrissy had to shower me, which was awful. To hide the fact that I was incredibly upset, we were all laughing about how helpless I was. I knew if I really thought about it, I'd be hysterical. After they left, and I got into bed, I was all alone. The only thing I could think about was my career at UConn being over. My tears began to flow again, and I don't remember them stopping. I cried, and cried, and cried some more.

I honestly think the Carrier Dome is cursed. My sophomore year I sprained my ankle when we played at Syracuse. It swelled up like a balloon, and I couldn't bear weight on it. I had to miss two games, which were the only two I ever missed in my career. Tonight I was in almost the exact same location on the floor, and I hurt my knee. How weird is that?

A couple of my teammates said before the game, "Remember what happened here?" joking around about my ankle. People always say to knock on wood when someone talks about getting hurt, or that playing on crutches is bad luck. I never paid attention to any of that stuff, but I believe it all now. I don't know if it is superstition or if the Carrier Dome is just an evil, evil building.

When TyTy's stepmom called me after the game to check on me, I said playfully, "I hate Syracuse and everyone from here! I'm never coming back!"

She said, "What if you marry my stepson? You better come back here!"

"Nope! Never!"

I'm going to try to get some sleep, but my guess is that I'll be up all night.

WEDNESDAY, JANUARY 16, 2008

I couldn't have slept for more than a few minutes. When my eyes opened, my hands went straight for my knee. I was hoping my injury was just a bad dream, but when I felt the fluid in my knee, I knew the nightmare was reality. Again, a wave of emotions swept over my body—disbelief, sadness, anger, and disappointment. I didn't want it to be real. I couldn't get out of bed and face the world. I just wanted to hide under my covers for the rest of my life.

This morning, Coach called to see how I was doing. I guess he needed a night to let everything sink in because he was really good about the whole situation. Last night, not only did he have to deal with my injury, but a terrible team performance as well. Without knowing the extent of my injury, it had to be very difficult for him to find the right things to say. I sure didn't know what to do the night of Kalana's injury. There is really nothing one can say to make it better. I had an MRI scheduled later in the day, so nothing was definite yet. Coach was trying to be optimistic. He said, "It might not be that bad."

"Yes, it is," I replied.

"You don't know that. Just wait and see what the MRI says. It might be something minor."

"No it's not. It's broken."

"What do you mean, 'it's broken'?"

"I mean it doesn't work. My knee is broken."

Coach was trying to keep my spirits up, but it wasn't working. I knew my knee was torn, and even if I tried to convince myself otherwise, it wouldn't change the facts.

First, my mom and Rosie and I went to see a team physician. He tried to examine my knee, but I had trouble relaxing because I hate the way the ACL test feels. Doctors and athletic trainers perform a standard test to determine if there is an ACL tear. They hold onto the leg just above the knee with one hand

and then just below the knee with the other. They stabilize the top portion and pull the bottom forward. If there's a lot of movement on the injured knee compared to the other knee, the ligament is usually damaged. The doctor kept telling me to relax, but my body was incredibly tense with fear. He performed the test on both legs, and said "Your right ACL doesn't seem too much looser than your left one. You may have just stretched it a little. You're really tense; I'm not sure if you are letting me get a good exam, but I don't think you tore your ACL."

"Really?" I asked. I was stunned.

"Mel, this is good news," he said. I was in complete shock. I had been convinced that my UConn basketball career was over.

"It might be just your meniscus, which can be as short as a four-week recovery. You could be back for the tournament." I was so excited; I couldn't believe what I was hearing. When I left the hospital, I reached for my cell phone and started texting everyone. Rosie called Tonya and told her the good news; and I texted Ketia, TyTy, and my dad.

Next, we drove to the office of Dr. Joyce, who is an orthopedic surgeon. I sat on the table, and he carried out the exact same test on me. Ten seconds later, he told me that he was 90-95 percent sure that I tore my ACL. My dreams were shattered again! My eyes got a little watery. I'm surprised I didn't start sobbing right there. Everything Dr. Joyce said to me after that was a blur. After the words "torn ACL" came out of his mouth, nothing else mattered.

I still had to get X-rays and an MRI to confirm the exact damage to my knee. I hobbled into the X-ray room right across the hall. The X-ray technician placed my leg and took a few pictures. Then she looked at me and asked, "Are you okay? You look really pale.'"

"I don't know. I'm really hot," I replied as I tore off my sweatshirt. I had been dizzy for a couple of minutes, but I didn't want to complain. I almost fainted, and I had to lie down for a minute. I don't know if it was the shock, the pain, or the disappointment, but I was a mess.

I felt really bad because Dr. Joyce tried to be so nice and helpful, but I wasn't my normal, cheerful self. I was so angry, upset, and surprised all at once that I didn't know what to feel. I just became numb. Dr. Joyce started to show me pictures about the procedure to fix my knee, but they made me want to vomit. I've never been okay with looking at blood and guts, which is kind of strange because my mom and my cousin are nurses, and so was my grandmother before she passed away. I told him I didn't want to see any of it and that I trusted he knew better than I did. I just wanted to get out of there as soon as possible, but I wasn't yet finished with doctors. I still had to go to a different hospital for an MRI. It wasn't so bad, though. I dozed off and was sound asleep the entire time, probably because I didn't sleep a wink the night before.

THURSDAY, JANUARY 17, 2008

I'm a little apprehensive about surgery. I'm sure I'll be fine, but it's always scary. I have had surgery twice before—first when I was a toddler, which I don't remember, and again my freshman year of college. I broke my nose, and it was moved a long way from where it was supposed to be. I remember that day like it was yesterday. I was playing defense on Stacey Marron and the coaches kept yelling, "Get up! Get up!" They wanted me to pressure the ball, so I moved closer and closer into her body. All of a sudden, her elbow ripped right through my face. I held my nose for a second in reaction to the initial shock, but I kept playing until I noticed blood dripping from my nose. I ran off the court to get tissues from the bathroom. By the time I reached the doors, my nose was gushing blood. It was smeared all over my face, and running down my arms into a large pool on the floor. I had never seen that much blood before; it looked like I killed somebody! By this time, Rosie made it to my rescue. She said, "Yea, well it looks like you broke your nose!"

I was laughing hysterically, saying "Look how much I'm bleeding!" I don't know why I thought it was so funny, and neither did Rosie, "What's wrong with you!" she said with a chuckle. That was the third time I broke my nose, so it didn't seem like such a big deal to me.

I'm a little more worried about knee surgery. It's much more serious. I've been icing my knee all day to reduce the swelling enough to allow for surgery. If there's too much inflammation, surgery is postponed until it subsides. My right knee was only slightly bigger than my left, so the doctor scheduled my operation for Friday, three days after the injury.

FRIDAY, JANUARY 18, 2008

I was anxious when I woke up this morning. Then, things got worse. My mom and I got lost on the way to the hospital, so I was afraid I'd be late. When we finally found the hospital, the receptionist checked me in, and sent me on to the pre-op room. I had to take off all my clothes and put on one of those cute hospital gowns that never cover your butt. My mom and Dr. Trojian, our team physician, were back there with me.

The anesthesiologist came in to put me under before surgery. When they gave me the medicine, they told me I wouldn't remember anything that happened, but I didn't believe them. They put me on a medicine called Versed, which makes a person completely goofy. Dr. Trojian and my mom later filled me in on all the ridiculous things I said.

"Hey guys! Talk to me!" I said to Dr. Trojian and my mom.

"Well, what would you like to talk about?" Dr. Trojian asked.

"Let's talk politics." They were both cracking up because I typically don't talk about politics for fun. "I've been following the election, so I know all about it," I told them.

"Well, what do you know?"

"Well there's Obama, and he's a black man, and there's Hillary, and she's a woman."

"Wow, you do know everything!"

That apparently was the extent of my profound knowledge of the election. I knew the race and gender of two of the Democratic candidates!

Next, I wanted to meet everyone there. I asked all the nurses and doctors what their names were, and I even made up nicknames for some of them.

The anesthesiologist warned me, "Now when we give you the drugs that put you to sleep, we're going to have you count backwards from 100 until you fall asleep."

I said, "I don't want to count backwards from 100; that will take too long. But you wanna know what I can do backwards? I can say the alphabet."

The anesthesiologist played along with me and said, "Oh yea? Let's hear you do it."

"Z-Y-X-W-V-U-T-S-R-Q-P-O-N-M-L-K-J-I-H-G-F-E-D-C-B-A"

"Wow, that's impressive, Mel."

"I know! But that's not all. I have lots of other special talents, too. I can make a swan out of paper. Get me a napkin. I'll make one for you!"

One of the nurses got me a napkin, but by that time I was so drugged up I had no idea what I was doing. I don't think I ever finished my masterpiece for the doctor, but as they wheeled me down the hall I was still trying to fold the napkin into a swan.

Right before I passed out on the operating table, I told Dr. Joyce, "Make sure you fix my meniscus if you can. I'm gonna need it someday!" I tore my meniscus, in addition to my ACL. Often, a torn meniscus can't be repaired. In this case, the damaged portion is cut out and removed, and the athlete is able to play with what is left. Apparently, I wanted to keep all of mine.

After surgery, I was supposed to be asleep, but instead I awoke in a panic. The nurse said, "Now you need to get some rest. Go back to sleep, okay?"

"You need to bring my mom back here so she can see that I'm okay," I said.

"She can come see you when you wake up."

"No, I need her to come back now. She worries about everything, and I want her to know I'm okay. Then I'll go back to sleep, I promise!" My mom came back to check on me, and then I did go to sleep. Surgery wasn't so bad after all. I actually had a lot of fun! The medication made it quite interesting.

SATURDAY, JANUARY 19, 2008

Today we played Cincinnati in Hartford. The doctors told me I probably shouldn't attend the game because my surgery was only yesterday. I was pretty drugged up from the medication, but I knew there was no way I wouldn't make it. Even if I was passed out in the stands, I would be there. Nothing could stop me from being with my teammates. I sat behind the bench so no one would bump my knee. It was propped up on a couple of pillows, and I had an ice machine on my leg. I don't remember much from the game because I was incredibly loopy from my painkillers. I knew we were winning by a large margin the entire game, so I had nothing to worry about.

I talked with my former teammate, Nicole Wolff, for a really long time today. She called to check on me and make sure I wasn't on a suicide watch.

Nicole tore her ACL when she was a sophomore, so she knows how it feels. When she called I was extremely happy, talking up a storm and laughing about everything. "Well I'm glad you're doing okay Mellie. I thought you would be a little more depressed," she said with a laugh.

"Oh, I'm feeling great right now!" I responded.

"Is that the painkillers talking?"

"Probably, but I've never been better!"

Every other person that called was shocked at my upbeat mood. Just about all my former UConn teammates called to see how I was doing, which meant a great deal to me.

The school has allowed me to stay in the Nathan Hale Hotel on campus until I can move around a little better. My school apartment is on the third floor, and there is no way I could hobble up and down so many steps on crutches and medication. Thankfully, my mom is staying in the hotel with me. I have to ice my knee throughout the night, so she sets an alarm that wakes her every hour in order to turn the ice machine on and off. I don't know what I would do if she weren't here.

CHAPTER 11
Baby Steps

SUNDAY, JANUARY 20, 2008

Today was my first day of rehab. It's unbelievable how much muscle I've lost in just a few days. One of my exercises is to do leg lifts. It takes everything in my power to lift my leg an inch off the ground. Another exercise is quad sets, which is simply flexing my quadriceps. I don't have enough strength in my leg to even contract the muscle. When Rosie told me to flex it, I stared in disbelief as absolutely nothing happened. "Go ahead," she said, not knowing I had been trying for 10 seconds. "I am!" I replied. It's becoming evident that the road in front of me is very long.

Showering is another ordeal. I'm not allowed to get my incisions wet. In order to keep them dry, I cover them with clear, sticky patches called Tegaderm. I can't put any pressure on my leg yet, so I have to hop on one foot to the bathtub. The hotel has provided me with a handicapped chair for the shower because I can't stand on one foot long enough to get clean. I can't reach anything, so I have to call my mom into the bathroom every time I need the soap, the shampoo, or the conditioner. My mom does just about everything but wash me herself!

MONDAY, JANUARY 21, 2008

In the early stages, bending the knee, or flexion, is vital to full recovery. Scar tissue can form quickly inside the knee and limit mobility, so it's crucial to spend time moving it each day. I lie on my stomach, and Rosie forces my knee to flex until it's uncomfortable. To measure the angle of flexion, she uses a goniometer, which is a tool that looks like a big protractor. A normal knee flexes past 135 degrees, but mine only bends to 86 degrees. It hurts a whole lot, and it feels like my knee is about to rip.

Tonight we played North Carolina at Gampel. We have had a great rivalry with them in recent years, and they are currently ranked number three in the country. This was an enormous test for us as we are still adjusting to playing without two of our starters. Before the game, I was presented with my recognition ball for scoring 1,000 points. As I walked onto the court, applause erupted from the sold-out arena. I was deeply moved by the tremendous show of support from the crowd. Every time Kalana and I walk out from the locker room, the fans cheer for us. This demonstrates their concern for us as people, not just players contributing to a win.

Coach presenting my 1,000-point ball

Maya soaring over North Carolina defenders

North Carolina jumped out to an 8-0 lead, led the entire first half, and was winning by 11 at halftime. I knew we needed a spark from somewhere if we were going to win the game. From behind the bench, I called Charde over to me. "Char, come on. You got this. Go out there and play like you know you can." She looked at me with fire in her eyes and nodded her head. I turned to Kalana and told her Charde was going to step up. I can tell just by looking into her eyes if I can trust her or not. Tonight, I knew I could trust her. She had a look of determination, and she scored 15 points in the second half. I was incredibly proud of her. Renee scored 26, including her 1,000th point. We ended up winning 82-71. All through the second half, Gampel Pavilion was the most electric I have ever seen it. The packed student section was so loud I could hardly talk to Kalana though she was sitting right next to me.

141

Photo courtesy of UConn Athletic Communications

The harder the battle, the sweeter the win

TUESDAY, JANUARY 22, 2008

Today, my knee bent 90 degrees in rehab. It has been an adventure trying to trek around campus in two inches of snow on crutches. Every time I went into a building, the rubber tips on my crutches were wet from the snow, so I slipped and slid everywhere. I almost fell three different times!

I finally moved back into my apartment, but I still need crutches, so it's very difficult to get around. It's a 10-minute process just to get up and go to the bathroom. The television in my room is a hand-me-down from Ann. The remote got lost somewhere along the way, so I have to hobble over to the television to change the channel. My mom didn't think it was a good idea, so she ordered me a new flat-screen TV with a remote. This is a big upgrade because the old one still had a VCR player in it. The day before, when I came back from rehab there was an iPod waiting for me on my bed. I've never had one before, so all my teammates have been teasing me for still carrying around a CD player. My mom is devastated for me, so she keeps buying me new toys in an attempt to lift my spirits. I know she just wants me to be able to play, but that's impossible, so I guess buying electronic equipment is the next best thing!

FRIDAY, JANUARY 25, 2008

Our student athletic trainer, Lindsey McDowell, told me today I had to walk a whole lap around the outside of Gampel. My eyes opened wide with fear. I had barely walked a step since leaving the hospital only one week ago. I didn't feel ready at all. It may sound silly to be scared to walk, but I don't trust my leg yet. Lindsey must have sensed my anxiety, "It's okay. You can do it," she said. She walked by my side the entire way, assuring me she was there if I needed help. I was holding back tears with each step. I just wanted it to be over, but it took an incredibly long time with all my baby steps. When I finally returned to the locker room, I had to do mini-squats for the first time. As I started to bend my knees, a wave of fear swept through my body. I was afraid my leg would collapse. I frantically looked at Lindsey and shook my head. "I can't do this." The tears I had been holding back finally began to flow. Lindsey handed me a tissue and let me calm down for a minute. It probably took a half hour to do 10 reps, but we finally got through them.

When I returned to my room tonight after rehab, my leg was throbbing with pain. Rosie told me I should ease off the painkillers, but my knee hurt so much that I just had to have some Vicodin. My prescription was at CVS, so I had Brit rush me there. Brit has been an amazing help to me through this whole ordeal. She's been through all of this herself, so she knows how awful it is. Since my mom went back to Cincinnati, Brit has been the one carrying my bags, filling my ice machine, and wrapping my leg. I love her!

Brit is also from Ohio, so I have known her for a long time. Not only did we play against each other in high school, but we also played for the same AAU organization. Brit scored 38 points on my high school team, but it wasn't enough because I made a game-winning shot over her outstretched arm at the buzzer. She'll argue differently, of course, claiming the shot wasn't on her, but we can find the game film somewhere! I tease her about it all the time, even though the game meant absolutely nothing—except that I'll have bragging rights for the rest of my life.

Brit was a phenomenal player coming out of high school and was named Player of the Year by *Parade* magazine. She wanted to attend UConn, but her parents insisted she go to Duke. One year and two knee surgeries later, she transferred to UConn, where the doctors performed a rare procedure that surgically placed a cadaver's meniscus in her injured knee. Because of the surgery and transfer, she had to redshirt during my freshman year. The first couple of years, her knee bothered her sporadically, but she continued to participate fully in practices and games. She was a gym rat and the person always willing to work out with me in the summertime. During the off-season, Brit and I were the best two-on-two duo on campus. We challenged anyone and everyone to play against us, and the football players were often our victims. I'm not sure what our overall record is, but it's almost perfect.

As the years passed, Brit's knee got worse and worse. Over time, her meniscus slowly deteriorated, so now she's almost running bone on bone again. She tried to push through it, but every time she did, the next day her knee was so sore she could barely run. The medical staff realized the only option was to limit the time she played on it. The athletic trainers began timing her minutes on the court each day. She is allowed to actively play basketball for only 15 minutes both in practices and in games. It's not unusual for her to score 10 points and grab seven boards in less than 15 minutes on any given night. Imagine what she could do if she played a whole game! Life has certainly not been fair to Brit. She plays harder and with more passion than anyone I know. She never feels sorry for herself, and she has handled her injury with patience and a good spirit. She makes the best of her minutes and provides a huge spark for our team whenever she's in the game.

Brit finally began to understand her limitations, but at first, it was hard for her. At one point, she was told by the medical staff that she couldn't play unless she wore her knee brace. Like any hardheaded athlete, Brit didn't want to wear it. She thought it was uncomfortable and restricting, so she threw it to the side one day while running down the court. When Renee realized what Brit was doing, she yelled, "Big Girl, put that brace back on!"

"Nah, I'm good," she responded.

"You're not playing unless you put that brace on."

"Let's go. I'm fine."

Renee ran over to Brit, slapped the ball out of her hands, and ran off the court with the ball. "How you gonna play now? You don't have a ball!"

Brit said, "Renee, stop being obnoxious! I can play. Relax!"

"You're so hardheaded! No one's playing until you put that thing on!"

It took a lot of convincing, but eventually Brit gave in and wore the brace. We all do dumb things from time to time, but when 13 other people are saying you're an idiot, you have no choice but to do the right thing.

It's doubtful Brit will be able to play professional ball because of her knee. She is interested in so many other things that I'm confident she'll be successful in life.

SATURDAY, JANUARY 26, 2008

Yesterday, Rosie had me shoot during rehab to work on my balance. She was grinning from ear to ear when she told me about the exercise. She understands how much I love basketball and just knew I'd be eager to shoot again. When she passed me the ball, it was the first time my hands had touched a basketball since my injury 11 days ago. With the first shot I took, I was overcome with anger. It wasn't supposed to happen like this. I looked out at the court and saw my teammates effortlessly running up and down, and then I glanced down at my giant knee brace. I stopped what I was doing and dropped the ball. "Are you okay?" Rosie asked. She must have seen the disappointment in my face.

"I really just don't want to be out here," I replied.

"It's fine. Are you sure you're okay?"

"I just wanna play, and this is making me depressed. I can't be out here. I don't want to touch a basketball again for a long time."

"I'm sorry. I didn't mean to upset you. I thought you'd be excited to get back on the court."

"So did I," I said as I crutched away from the game I love, and went back to the training room.

SUNDAY, JANUARY 27, 2008

We played Notre Dame today at the Joyce Center. They are ranked sixteenth in the country. Maya had the first 15 points in the opening four minutes of the game, and we won 81-64. Maya is ridiculously good. Now that I can't play, I have time to just sit back and watch her every day. She is an amazing athlete.

THURSDAY, JANUARY 31, 2008

Last night we played South Florida in Hartford. They were 1-6 in the league. The game was awful. We looked really lethargic, like we didn't want to be out there. The post players were terrible, and Coach benched all of them in the second half. Tina didn't start after halftime and played only two minutes total in the second half. Coach said, "Some players are great and play bad every once in a while; and then there are players who are mediocre and play great every once in a while—and that's what you are." We can always count on Coach to give it to us straight. We know he's not going to sugarcoat anything for us. He tells Tina almost every day that she's "the worst post player in America" because he knows she has the potential to be the best post player in the country.

Tina isn't the first UConn player to hear those words. When Rebecca Lobo was a freshman, Coach was always telling her she was "the worst post player in America." By the time she graduated, she was a First Team All-American and National Player of the Year. She won the 1995 National Championship with UConn, and later an Olympic gold medal with Team USA.

Although Tina gets harassed every day, she will someday emerge stronger than she ever thought she could be. She listens, and she wants to improve. Every day she comes to the gym early to do extra workouts with CD. If players have a desire to be the best, Coach will find a way to help them make it happen. It may be a rough road, but eventually they get there. Tina's not there yet, but she's on the journey.

For the majority of the second half, five guards were on the floor: Lorin, Ketia, Renee, Maya, and Megs. In the 11 minutes that Megs was in the game, she was the leading rebounder and had as many offensive rebounds as Charde, Tina, Kaili, and Brit combined. Coach wasn't too happy that South Florida outrebounded us. During one of the time-outs, Coach said, "You guys think this is a joke? Because I don't. I'm serious about what we're doing here. You want to see how serious I am? You'll find out at 6:00 a.m. tomorrow how serious I am."

After the game, Coach walked slowly into the locker room and said calmly, "I don't have much to say. Everything I need to say will be said tomorrow morning at 6:00 a.m." And with that he walked out.

FRIDAY, FEBRUARY 1, 2008

Everyone was at the gym bright and early for our 6:00 a.m. practice today. During practice, Kalana and I were in the training room doing rehab, and one of the managers walked in. I asked, "How is it out there?"

She replied, "Well Kaili, Charde, and Tina just finished their seventeenth suicide of the day if that says anything." Usually, our conditioning comes from sprinting hard through every drill. Coach rarely makes us get on the line and run sprints, unless we really tick him off. Practices are usually fun, and we enjoy being there, but today wasn't one of those days.

We all went to class for a couple of hours and returned to the gym for the second practice at 1:30. After it ended, everyone looked dead tired when they came back to the locker room. Just walking looked painful for them. I felt awful that I wasn't out there with them. We share the good times together, as well as the bad times, but I'm not part of it anymore.

SUNDAY, FEBRUARY 3, 2008

This sucks. I miss playing basketball more than I ever could have imagined. It's like my whole world has been turned upside-down. I don't feel involved in anything anymore. I'm constantly in the training room removed from my team. I don't see much of practice, so I'm oblivious to what happens every day. I can't even sit on the bench because I'm still in my brace. I'm clueless as to what is said during the huddles. I am just an outsider now. Each time they break a huddle, I listen to the faint sound of my teammates yelling, "Together," but we're not all together. In the locker room, when my teammates laugh about something that happened in practice, I feel left out. Not only has basketball been taken away, but my boyfriend is also on the other side of the country. The two things I love most are just gone!

CHAPTER 12
Not So Perfect

WEDNESDAY, FEBRUARY 6, 2008

It's 12:30 a.m. We're on our way back from Rutgers. We lost! At the beginning of the year, I envisioned a perfect season. Now it's out the window. We were winning by nine at halftime, but they simply outplayed us in the second half—beating us by two. I felt helpless. I was so distant from my team, sitting by myself off in the stands. I couldn't even encourage my teammates because I was too far away. Kalana has been cleared to sit on the bench for a while now but she has stayed with me, so I wouldn't have to be alone. But for this game, the seats Rutgers gave us weren't together, so she sat on the bench.

After the game, I walked off the court and the Rutgers fans yelled all kinds of horrible things at me: "How does it feel that your last game at the Rac is a loss?" "Sucks you couldn't lose with them, Thomas!" or "Too bad your career is over!" I tried to ignore them, but they were screaming obnoxiously and were completely rude.

Coach came in the locker room much calmer than I expected. He said, "Charde, you've already checked out on us haven't you? What did your away message (on AIM) say the other day? Did any of you guys read it? It said, 'I can't wait 'til this chapter of my life is over.' And when I asked her about it, she told me it had to do with something going on at home. Do you think that's true? I think its bull. That wasn't up there until the day of the 6:00 a.m. practice."

We often communicate online on AOL Instant Messenger (AIM). When users are away from their computers, they can put messages up for all their buddies to see. Apparently, Coach read Charde's away message, which said she couldn't wait for this chapter of her life to be over. I didn't read it. At this point, I had no idea what was going on. Coach usually stays out of our personal lives, unless he suspects something is affecting what we do on the court. So this must have been serious.

He asked me in front of everybody, "Do you think it was about something other than basketball?"

"I honestly don't know," I responded. I don't know what is going on in Charde's personal life. I wouldn't be the least bit surprised if it was about basketball, but I wasn't going to say I knew that for a fact.

Coach said to Charde, "Until further notice, this chapter of your life *is* over." That was a little drastic, but I think Coach is tired of Charde's antics. For four years, from one day to the next, he hasn't known what to expect from her. He's finally fed up.

What makes Charde's inconsistent performances so frustrating is that she has enormous talent. When she is in the right frame of mind, she can be the best player on our team and arguably in the country. Charde holds the high school scoring record in California—3,837 points. She broke Cheryl Miller's record, and Diana Taurasi is third on the list. Charde has the ability to dominate every game she plays in. Sadly, in her four years at UConn, she has only shown occasional moments of brilliance, as in the second half of the North Carolina game this year.

Charde wasn't the only one who received Coach's wrath tonight. He said to Maya, "You're half the problem, Maya Moore. You don't play defense or rebound; all you wanna do is stand out there and shoot threes."

The difference is that Maya would take that to heart and do something about it, while Charde would just let Coach defeat her. Coach does everything for a reason. It's to make us better, to make us stronger. He always tells us, "If you can beat me, you can beat anybody. There are going to be times when we're on the road, and we have the other team, their crowd, and maybe even the refs against us. If you can't even beat me, do you think you're going to come out on top in that situation?" He's completely right. There are times in some games when nothing goes our way. The things we do every day in practice prepare us for those moments.

A very focused Charde Houston

In practice, Coach often puts us in situations that are almost impossible to beat. He has us start 10 points down with five minutes to play, and we have to overcome the deficit. Coach puts a bubble on the other team's basket, which is like putting a lid on it. It fits on top of the hoop, so no shot can go in and all shots can be rebounded. Every ball that hits the bubble counts as a score for the other team, and they also receive points for rebounding their own "misses." So basically, they score on every shot attempt and offensive rebound. The only way we can score is to actually make a basket. It sounds impossible to win in this situation, but we've accomplished it. Coach even makes us play five against eight. If we can guard eight people, five becomes a piece of cake. Everything we do tests us mentally. If we don't think we can do it, there's no way we can. Sometimes we believe we can prevail, but we still lose. Then, there are times when we do beat the odds, and we feel we can do anything.

As a senior, Charde still doesn't understand that Coach challenges us for good reasons. Too often Charde doesn't buy into what Coach is saying, so she thinks he's just out to get her. On the other hand, when Coach gets on Maya, she uses it as motivation. Maya has a toughness about her, which is why she will continue to get better. Although she didn't play her best game by any stretch of the imagination, she never gave up and she got us back in the game—making three 3s in the last four minutes.

After Coach left the locker room, I went to the bathroom and bawled in a stall by myself for at least 10 minutes. On the way back, CD talked to me on the bus. She asked me to take on a leadership role off the court. When I was playing, Renee and I split the responsibilities. Now that I'm not out there, Renee has a lot more to worry about. CD said, "Renee is in charge of everything on the court on her own. If she's concerned with off-court responsibilities, too, I think she's going to end up emotionally drained. I want you to try taking some of that off her shoulders."

Before I got hurt, there was a good balance between Renee and me. I was always enthusiastic and upbeat, pushing everyone to work hard. She was the one that put people in their place when they weren't doing what was expected of them. Without me out there, I'm sure it's harder on her, so I'm going to help more in that area.

WEDNESDAY, FEBRUARY 6, 2008

I spent much of today thinking about CD's advice. I know there are many specific ways I can still contribute to my team. I remember how hard it could be to deal with Coach when I was a freshman, so I asked Maya how she's doing. She was pretty upset over the Rutgers loss and disappointed with herself that she couldn't figure out a way to beat them. Maya *hates* to lose, but adversity clearly motivates her and makes her stronger. Her maturity level far exceeds that of most freshmen.

The next person I talked to was Kaili. She approached me after the game last night and gave me a big hug. She said, "I'm sorry we couldn't keep it perfect for you." She loves basketball, so it sucks to see her frustrated. She likes to do things her way and is as stubborn as I used to be whenever people tell her that her way is the wrong way. She'll be okay, though, because she wants to get better.

The person I am really worried about is Charde. She never opens up, so it's extremely hard to have a conversation with her. I tried talking to her over the internet today because the last time I tried to speak with her in person, I almost strangled her.

"How are you doin'? You alright?" I asked.

"No, I'm not okay. I'm not happy. Everything I do is wrong. It's kind of a lose/lose situation," she responded.

"I know you don't like talking about anything, but I wish you would. Are you okay? Is there anything I can do to help you? Do you wanna play, honestly? I mean, do you still even like basketball?"

"I love basketball, but I hate it right now, and why wouldn't I? I tell myself it will get better, but it doesn't seem like it will."

"I know Coach is hard on you, but it's only because he wants to make you better. I can see how that might have gotten messed up for you, but do you think you still have anything left?"

"I feel like I have a lot left, but I'm so overwhelmed."

"At this point you can either put everything you have into finishing this year or you can say 'forget it.' I would love to see you enjoy playing again, like you did in the Carolina game. It's not all on your shoulders. You don't have to feel this pressure to do everything perfectly, just give your best and keep a positive attitude."

"Yea, that's what I want to do. I was mad because that away message was up way before practice. I feel like I have to be perfect or stuff like this happens."

"I don't know anything about the away message. I don't know the situation, and that's why I didn't say anything in the locker room, but forget that. That's not what this is about. That's just something that got thrown in because of everything else that's happened. If you had scored 20 points in a win, it wouldn't have been an issue. But that's not even important. It's what's left that matters. I just want to see you happy and enjoy the rest of the season. I would give anything to get back out there, and you are still blessed to be doing something you love. You just have to show what you're made of, and overcome all this. I know you can, and you know you can. It's just whether you want to or not. You can be great, or you can give up. It's up to you."

"You're right, and I want to do it."

"You've got to honestly commit to it, Charde. Get in the gym by yourself and find your love for the game. In just two more months, you will be done playing basketball at UConn forever. I hope you can look back and feel like you accomplished something. If you don't honestly want to do that, just tell everyone on the team what you have left and what you can give. If you're not able to put everything into it, don't say you will. Just be honest with all of us. I'll do anything to help you; just please let me know. These are our last few months together."

"Okay, I understand. Thanks so much!"

Did anything change? Did anything get through to her? I don't know. I don't have any idea. I hope so.

Charde had a meeting with Coach today, and then went straight to our team film session. I'm assuming she straightened things out with him. We watched the entire Rutgers game from last night. Like it wasn't bad enough to watch it once, I had to replay all my emotions again. It took hours to re-watch the entire game. Coach held all the power in the world in his little rewind button. We watched certain plays at least 10 times. It's awful to make a stupid mistake in the game, but it's much worse to know it's on tape and Coach can play it over and over again.

After Coach reamed out almost every player, he said, "We have a problem because people don't own this. They just borrow it for a couple years and then throw it back. It never truly becomes part of who they are. That's why our program has been different than others. Once you're a part of this family, you are connected for life. Then there are some people who just take, take, take, and never give back. We know who those people are because once they're gone, they're gone. We never see or hear from them again. How many people on our team do you think live, breathe, and sleep Connecticut Basketball? If it's not most of our guys, then we're in trouble."

I don't actually sleep Connecticut Basketball, but I sure do live it. Nothing makes me happier than to be a part of this program, where I have fun winning games alongside people I love. I want to add my name to the list of great players who have won a National Championship here. Nothing in the world would be more fulfilling.

CHAPTER 13

Back on Solid Ground

SATURDAY, FEBRUARY 9, 2008

Today we had a game at Seton Hall. With three of their best players hurt, it wasn't much of a contest. We all squeezed into a tiny locker room before the game listening to Coach's pregame speech. I began thinking about how much I missed playing and started getting a little teary-eyed. I was off to the side, so I didn't think anyone saw me. As we left the locker room, Kalana said right in front of Coach, "Why are you crying?"

Trying to hide my emotions, I said, "I'm not crying. What are you talking about?" I just miss playing so much, and sometimes it hits me that I will never play another game for UConn. I always knew how much I loved basketball, but I never thought I would be this affected by not being able to play.

THURSDAY, FEBRUARY 14, 2008

I had to ride the bike during rehab today. As I frantically pedaled to keep up with the program, I heard the loudest pop in my knee. I screamed, and everyone in the training room turned to look at me. Lindsey and Rosie ran to my rescue. They assured me it was only the scar tissue in my knee breaking up, but I freaked out. It's been a rough day. To make matters worse, it's Valentine's Day. Everyone is walking around campus with roses and teddy bears, but my Valentine is 3,000 miles away!

FRIDAY, FEBRUARY 15, 2008

For players with injuries, the trainers often have us do pool rehab because it puts less pressure on our joints than running. Today for rehab, I jogged in the pool for the first time. It felt great to run, even if it was in the water!

In order to stay in shape, Kalana and I do 45 minutes of cardio each day. Our choices are the bike, the Stairmaster, or the elliptical. I hate them all. Not only are they tedious and monotonous, but they're hard! I used to think exercise machines were a joke, but I sure was wrong. Rosie makes us do intense, high-level programs, and I always get an urge in my finger to press the Level Down button about five times. I never do, though, because I want to get back into playing shape as quickly as possible. I also schedule extra lifting workouts with Coach West, which are more enjoyable.

After practice, a few of my teammates posed for Cassie's photo project. Renee, Megs, T, Ketia, and I were her models. She painted different designs on our faces, and took pictures from different angles with different lighting. I don't understand all that artistic stuff. Modeling was actually harder than I imagined, but it was a lot of fun. Cassie is an art major and has extraordinary talent. I have

Models for a day: T, Ketia, me, and Megs

no idea how she does what she does. She goes from the studio to practice, then back to the studio. Cassie has had projects during which she doesn't sleep for days, and then she's expected to go to practice and perform. The huge amount of time she spends on her art truly pays off because her work is incredible. She can sketch a picture of anything and make it look as real as a photograph. I really admire what she does because I don't think there's any way I could live her lifestyle. I feel swamped with my schedule, but it's nothing compared to hers.

SATURDAY, FEBRUARY 16, 2008

After the blue team had been on the floor for almost three hours, they had to end practice by scoring five times in a row. I watched turnover after missed shot after turnover. Coach said, "I don't care if we stay until midnight." He sat down, crossed his legs, and just watched. He wanted to see if they were tough enough to finish the drill when they were dead tired. It took a while, but they refused to give up until they did it. Afterwards, he called us into the huddle and said, "Do you think there's gonna be a time when you have to get five scores in a row in March or April? What if they score five times in a row, and we have to match it each time? Maybe if we had Mel and Kalana, I'd feel like we had more room for error. With what we've got now, our margin for error is very small. I'm going to make it death camp every time you're in here. You can hate me, but whatever frustrations you have, you can take out on the teams we're playing. Where you guys want to go is a really hard thing to do. You have to decide if this is important enough that you're willing to fight for it every day. When we come out in the end, you'll be so much stronger."

Everyone is coming together. We've been through so much adversity that the people left on the court have had to mature in a short period of time. Much more pressure is added to their shoulders because they are all playing almost 40 minutes every night. I am really proud of our team because everyone is embracing this challenge.

SUNDAY, FEBRUARY 17, 2008

Today we played at Pittsburgh and won 90-64. At halftime of the game, Coach asked all of us, "What do Tina Charles and a dead person have in common?"

Everyone looked around at each other, confused. "They both have the same amount of defensive rebounds. Tina Charles is doing the same thing that a dead person is doing six feet under. Nothing! What's the point of having you out there?" I thought it was pretty hilarious. Really, though? A dead person! I don't think she found it too humorous, but being compared to a dead person motivated her enough to end up with 12 rebounds!

SUNDAY, FEBRUARY 24, 2008

Tonight was Senior Night. This is a UConn tradition that honors our graduating players and team managers before their last home game. The managers are honored first. They walk alongside their parents to half-court where they receive an achievement plaque. The players are next, and Coach gives us our framed jerseys. The fans show their appreciation for all the hard work and excitement each player has brought to the program. It's a very emotional night for everyone.

I can't believe four years have flown by so fast. I haven't been excited about Senior Night because I haven't wanted it to come. I don't want to graduate. I don't want to leave here. I feel it was just yesterday that Ketia and I were counting down the days until we could leave summer school and go back home. The summer before my freshman year, Ketia and I lived in dorms that were far away from our teammates and the gym. We didn't know anyone, and we absolutely hated it here. We both had long-distance boyfriends and were incredibly homesick. I came to UConn the day after my high school graduation. I wasn't ready to leave my family and my friends. Neither of our long-distance relationships survived and we found new boyfriends soon enough. At the time, however, leaving all this behind seemed like a big deal. We made a countdown calendar until the day we got to go home. Every night we'd look at each other and say, "You ready yet?"

"No, no, let's wait a little longer." The highlight of each day was finally crossing it off the calendar. We would run around the room and jump on the beds shouting for joy. We've come a long way since then. Ketia and I really latched on to each other our first year.

Throughout the entire basketball season, we never knew if we would start, or come off the bench, or not play at all. We had to deal with losing, the wrath of Coach, and being homesick. Some days it seemed everything was against us, but we had one another. We learned to stay strong together. The first few grueling months were worth it because I grew to love this place and call it my home.

One of the first times my mom visited me at school, I asked her, "Hey, Mom, can you take me home?"

"What did you just say?" she replied.

I looked at her confused and rephrased what I asked, "Um…I said can you take me to my dorm, please?"

She said, "Oh, okay. For a second there I thought you called this place your home."

I started laughing, and said, "No, Mom! Cincinnati's my home. I'm just staying here for a little while." I really meant what I said. I didn't want Connecticut to be my home, but here I am, looking back four years later, distraught I have to leave my home. I've formed bonds with my teammates that I'll carry with me the rest of my life. I truly value my time at this school and my experiences with the basketball program.

Three hours before the game, I started to get ready in the locker room. As I applied my mascara, tears were already streaming down my face. I realized eye makeup probably wasn't the best choice. I can't believe this is almost over. I live for UConn Basketball. It has become so large a part of who I am that I can't imagine doing anything else. All my dreams and desires are wrapped up in this program.

As much as I wanted to stop time, I couldn't. My name was called to walk out to center court with my mother and father. I felt so appreciative of them. They are the most encouraging parents anyone could ever have. The ceremony was very touching. I was sobbing my eyes out in the tunnel before I even walked onto the court. I was crying so hard I couldn't breathe. My mom was next to me, sobbing twice as hard as I was. Every time we looked at each other we'd laugh about how much we were crying. She said, joking around, "See, this is why I didn't want you to come to this stupid school! If you had stayed close to home, people wouldn't have cared as much, and this wouldn't be so sad!" When I hugged Coach, I started crying harder, if that was possible, but he told me everything was going to be fine.

Senior night with my mom and dad

The fans here are unlike anywhere else in the country. I feel so fortunate that we've had the support of so many people. The whole state loves us. Everyone on our team has a truly good heart, and they are always genuine and friendly with the public.

It's clear that Coach recruits "character first"—even before talent. The way some professional athletes and men's basketball players act is disappointing and sad. There was a time when those pros were little kids, looking up to some amazing athlete or role model. If a celebrity is rude to someone who admires him or her, the fan's perception of the individual and the team is diminished forever. People in the spotlight *are* role models, whether they want to be or not. I consider it an honor and never take that responsibility lightly.

We are given many opportunities at UConn to impact peoples' lives. I enjoy and treasure these opportunities.

After one game, a teenage girl approached me and asked for an autograph. She told me the strength and determination I demonstrated throughout my operation and recovery gave her the courage she needed to be brave through her own knee surgery.

Numerous older fans often tell me how much joy our team brings into their lives. They say we give them something to look forward to and bring excitement to their homes. One woman approached me and said, "My father passed away right before the season last year. You were the one thing that my mother had to look forward to and to live for. You were her favorite, and I don't know what she would have done in that time if she didn't have you."

One of my most rewarding experiences came when I met a young girl named Chelsea. My aunt met her through the website "The Boneyard" and learned she was an intense UConn basketball fan. Chelsea had a severe case of glaucoma, which required surgery to reduce the pressure on her eyes. She told my aunt how much she adored me, so my aunt arranged for me to visit her after surgery. I had never met the girl before, but I was eager to help. A friend from school, Katie Anderson, and I drove an hour to her house which was 40 miles from campus in the middle of farm country. When she opened the door, she couldn't believe I was really standing in front of her.

After she recovered from her initial shock, she gave me a tour of the house, ending up in her bedroom. It was amazing to see pictures of me covering her walls. She was completely star-struck for the first 15 minutes, not saying anything except, "I can't believe you're here." After visiting for a while at her house, we went to lunch at a local restaurant. After I dropped some food in my lap a few times, I think she understood I was just a regular person. She became more comfortable with the situation and began telling me about her life.

Chelsea had glaucoma since she was a baby and was adamant about raising awareness of the disease as well as fundraising to help researchers find a cure. She had always loved basketball, but her eyesight prevented her from playing, so she attended every high school practice and game as a manager. She was almost legally blind, but she never let that stop her from realizing her goals.

Katie, Chelsea, and me

She threw shot put for her high school track and field team, and accepted a scholarship from a small school.

I walked into Chelsea's home thinking I was doing a good deed and perhaps could inspire this young girl. Instead, I left several hours later completely in awe of her. She is a remarkable girl who hasn't let her disability limit her from anything. The disappointments and setbacks I've encountered in my life are nothing compared to hers. Most impressive is the grace with which she handles it all.

People have given me all kinds of gifts and mementos: scrapbooks, colored drawings, notes, and magnets. When I injured my knee, I was surprised at the hundreds of letters I received. I knew people cared, but I wasn't prepared for the magnitude of their concern. I attempted to respond to every letter because I was honored to be supported by so many kind people.

One of the best aspects of UConn Basketball is having opportunities to give back to the community that supports us. We often go to children's hospitals where the kids are always happy to see us. Brightening a sick child's day is always rewarding. We've volunteered at soup kitchens, and helped with Adopt-a-Family for the American Red Cross. We even went to the U.S. Embassy while we were in Italy and assisted with the kickoff of Toys for Tots. Being a part of this team involves much more than just playing basketball. I never imagined the many ways that UConn Basketball would change my life.

TUESDAY, FEBRUARY 26, 2008

Yesterday, we had a game at LSU. The last time we played them was to make it to the Final Four in last year's NCAA Tournament. We played the worst game of our season and were knocked out of the tournament. So, it was time for revenge. The game was way too close for my comfort. My stomach was tied in knots from start to finish. We were up only one point with 2:33 left in the game. Then Ketia made a huge three and we never looked back. I couldn't even move. I was paralyzed with my hands covering my face, but we won 74-69.

LSU has a beautiful campus in Baton Rouge. After shootaround, some of the players wanted to see the live tiger that's in a big fenced area by the arena. A couple of the younger guys thought we were trying to fool them. They didn't believe there was a real tiger on campus. I don't blame them, though, because our team often plays tricks on each other, and Renee is usually the ringleader.

Renee and I took a public speaking class together a couple of years ago. I spent hours and hours writing down notes and practicing each speech a dozen times. Renee would walk into the classroom, and I'd say, "You ready for your speech?"

"We *do* have a speech today, don't we?"

"Yes, Renee! Did you write your notes out?"

"No, I guess I could."

Completely unprepared, she would stand up in front of our class and speak like she was Martin Luther King Jr. She received better grades than I did on every single speech. She's the queen of BS'ing her way through any situation. She has a very strong personality and has the ability to convince anybody of anything. Sometimes she completely makes things up, just for the sheer joy of watching people believe her fiction. T is frequently the victim of Renee's jokes. T is the sweetest girl you could ever meet. She will do anything for anybody. She is also the most gullible person I've ever met. She believes everything she's told—no questions asked.

When T was a freshman, Renee told her there was a "Cat Party" at UConn where everyone dressed up as cats and had to perform a dance routine to be admitted to the party. Brit, Renee, and Kalana choreographed the dance, putting T in the front of the line so she couldn't see that she was the only one dancing. The whole time they taught her this ridiculous dance, she thought they were behind her doing the same thing. Instead, they were just laughing hysterically. They kept hyping her up, saying, "T, you have to get into it more." or "That's really good, T, we're definitely gonna win this year!" They performed the dance for everyone they saw, so by the end of the week, everyone was in on the joke. When she finally learned there was no "Cat Party," she was devastated—but she was able to laugh about it.

Nothing compares to the Super Bowl story. One day, Renee decided to tell T that the Super Bowl was going to be played on the UConn campus that year. The venue was a small (5,000-seat) stadium next to Gampel, where our football team used to play before their new stadium, Rentschler Field, opened. According to Renee, everyone on our team would receive a limited number of tickets. Charde added to the story by saying our team had been asked to do the halftime show. Again, T learned an entire routine which she thought she would perform at halftime of the Super Bowl.

The more T believed, the more excited Renee became. Renee claimed she had many family members coming to the game, so she asked for extra tickets from her teammates. T comes from a big family, so she started to worry about the limited supply. She frantically began asking her teammates if she could have their tickets to the Super Bowl. Renee warned us in advance, so we played along with the joke. T was distressed her family would miss the game, so she called her dad and explained the whole situation. He responded,

"Tahirah, the Super Bowl is not going to be on campus next year."

"Yes it is, Dad!"

Her dad tried to convince her that it wasn't true, but finally got annoyed after arguing with her and said sarcastically, "Fine, Tahirah. Get me a ticket."

Now that she had to get her dad a ticket, she was really on a mission. She asked every single player on the team, but we all added fuel to the fire, saying that we had already given ours to Renee. Renee had everyone on the team, even the coaches, in on this one. After T realized all the tickets were gone, she was furious. She stormed up to Renee and said, "I really don't think it's fair that you just took everyone's tickets! I have a lot of family members too, and it's only right that you share some of them with me!"

It took her entirely too long to figure out that we were playing a joke on her. After that, I don't think T ever believed another word out of Renee's mouth!

SATURDAY, MARCH 1, 2008

My heart is still pounding! We just beat DePaul by one. I sat there in shock as I watched my team fall to a 17-point deficit in the second half. But their spirits never got down, and they kept chipping away at the lead. With only 12 seconds to go, DePaul still had a one-point lead—and the ball in the open court on a breakaway play. It certainly looked like an easy layup for DePaul, and a loss for UConn that would cost us the Big East Championship.

But Maya was still fighting to win. She sprinted almost the whole length of the court, caught the DePaul player from behind, stole the ball, and called time-out. The game clock read six seconds. This was the most amazing defensive play I've ever seen. During the time-out, Coach drew up a play for Ketia to go coast to coast all the way to the basket. Ketia is the fastest player on our team and she executed the play perfectly—finishing with a beautiful scoop shot around two defenders, off the glass, and into the net. This put us up one with 1.6 seconds remaining.

As time expired, I jumped and ran out onto the court, neither of which I am cleared to do. But I couldn't help it. I was so excited! We deserved to lose that game the way we played in the first half; but there are two halves to a game. The last 20 minutes, my teammates fought like hell and found a way to win. Coach never lost confidence for a second, and neither did my teammates. As poorly as we played, we stuck together until the end.

MONDAY, MARCH 3, 2008

We beat Rutgers by 20 points tonight. I am so happy right now! I feel like we won the National Championship even though it was only the Big East Regular Season title. Before the game, our conference record was 14 -1. We came into the game tied with Rutgers in the Big East, so the winner of the game took the conference title.

Tonight's game was very physical, which is not unusual whenever we play Rutgers. One of their players fouled Maya extremely hard with just a few minutes left in the game. I think Maya's okay, but she went down awfully hard. With Ketia in foul trouble, Lorin was expected to contribute coming off the bench. She played great, and when she came off the court at the end of the game, Coach gave her a huge hug. My mom and Ketia's dad were joking around saying, "How many times did Coach hug Mel and Ketia their freshman year?" Honestly, though, I don't know that we ever gave him much reason to hug us when we were freshmen.

Kalana and I accept the Big East Regular Season trophy

When Coach told Kalana and me to accept the Big East trophy on behalf

165

of our team, I was honored. At that moment, any disappointment I had been feeling about not being able to play was completely outweighed by the pride I felt for my teammates. Right after my injury, I felt sorry for myself for a couple of weeks, but I soon realized that wouldn't do me any good. I came to UConn to be part of a team. Over the past month and a half, I have learned the true meaning of that. Never before in my life have I had to rely on other people more than I do right now. Fortunately, I have all the faith in the world in them.

Even though he has gotten technical fouls in two of the last three games, I have never seen Coach this calm before. He knows we're good; we know we're good; and everyone is acting like it. He told us we deserved this more than any other UConn team. I've never seen Coach so proud and so happy!

I was celebrating with my teammates in the apartment, when TyTy walked through the front door. He came back to Connecticut to surprise me! All his hard work paid off at the NFL Combine because he ran the fastest 40-yard dash time of all the defensive backs (4.31). It was the second fastest time of all 334 players. TyTy also placed in the top five of all defensive backs in the bench press. He benched 225 pounds 19 times. In his freshman year he couldn't bench that much once! I'm so proud of him. Now he just has to wait for the NFL draft in April.

I've spent my entire life at the center of what is happening around me. I was always the active one, the player, never the spectator. Now I'm living vicariously through all my friends. I couldn't be happier that the hard work of so many people I love is paying off. Sometimes life forces us to assume new and different roles. If we not only accept these roles, but truly embrace them, they can be extremely rewarding.

WEDNESDAY, MARCH 12, 2008

This weekend was the Big East Tournament. The top 12 teams in the league traveled to Hartford to compete for the championship. The weekend starts out with an awards dinner, which we dominated. Winning teams earn respect. Maya received the Big East Freshman of the Year award, as well as Big East Player of the Year. This is the first time in our league's history that a freshman has won that award. Ketia received the Sixth Man of the Year award and

All-Big East Honorable Mention. Maya, Renee, and Tina were all on the First Team. Coach was named Co-Coach of the Year, and Lorin was on the All-Freshman Team. I was so proud of my teammates!

In the first game of the tournament, we redeemed ourselves against DePaul by winning 86-67. Next, we played Pittsburgh in the semifinals, and prevailed 74-47. Finally, we advanced to the championship game against Louisville, who had shocked many people by beating Rutgers in the other semifinal match up. The game was extremely close, but we pulled it out 65-59. Charde played a phenomenal game—making play after play to help us win.

Celebrating after the Big East Tournament Championship

As the All-Tournament Team was being announced, I listened to name after name, waiting to hear "Charde Houston," knowing she absolutely deserved the recognition. As the announcer neared the end of the list, I turned to her and said, "Char Char, are you MVP?"

"No. No," she responded. The next thing we hear is, "And the Most Outstanding Player, Charde Houston, University of Connecticut." I had been so excited to see her play well, and I could not have been happier than to see her receive this honor. After all the adversity she has been through with UConn Basketball, I would love to see her go out on a positive note.

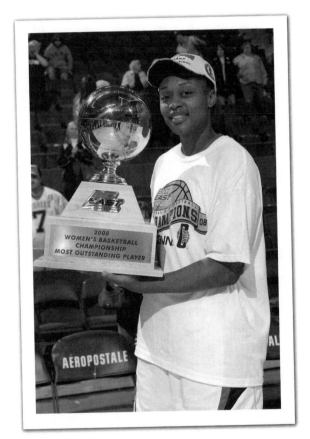

Charde is "Most Outstanding Player"

CHAPTER 14

The Last Dance

MONDAY, MARCH 17, 2008

It's that time of year again—NCAA Tournament time. Each Selection Show Monday, our team crowds around the television in the locker room to see our destiny unveiled. It's always exciting to learn who we are going to play and where. As the number-one seed, we were the first team announced as the brackets were revealed. When Rutgers's name appeared on the screen as the number-two seed in our bracket, my jaw dropped. I was completely surprised. The committee is supposed to pair the number-one overall seed with the worst number-two seed. I didn't think Rutgers was the worst number-two seed, and I never thought they would pair us with another Big East school. But those decisions are out of our control, and we have several games to win before we even think about facing them again. Coach's philosophy is that we should never worry about what team we're playing or what the other team is going to do. If we focus on what we do best, no other team can beat us. I think our team has that mentality and is very confident going into the tournament.

Although being the number-one seed in the tournament is exciting, it really doesn't mean a thing. We proved for the first 33 games that we were the best team in the country, but ultimately six games will define our season.

FRIDAY, MARCH 21, 2008

Today, we left for Bridgeport, Connecticut, where we play our first two tournament games. On the bus ride, we listened to most of the UConn men's game with San Diego State. This was their first-round game in the men's tournament. We had to catch the end of it at the restaurant where we ate dinner. Thirty of us crowded around one television, yelling at the screen.

Our point guard, A.J. Price, tore his ACL at the end of the first half. I want to cry for him. It made me sick to see it happen. It looks like Kalana and I will be getting a new training-room buddy. We all stood looking at each other in disbelief as the clock ran out and our fourth-seeded Huskies were upset by the thirteenth seed, San Diego State University. It just shows that anything can happen when March rolls around.

SATURDAY, MARCH 22, 2008

It's great that we're playing in Connecticut where our fan support is so strong. Hundreds of people came out today to watch our open practice. They went crazy when their Huskies ran onto the floor. While the rest of the team was stretching, I was shooting baskets. With every shot I made, the crowd erupted in applause. It was funny, because I was the only one on the court, but I actually felt like an athlete again.

We love our fans even when they do outrageous and entertaining things. At practice, there was an excited man yelling, "Myra! Myra! Look at this!" while holding up a newspaper article with MAYA printed in a huge font across the top. I don't know where the r is in her name, but this was not the first time a fan has called her "Myra." We like to tease her about it, so we often call her "Myra" now.

Tonight we went to a steakhouse called Carmen Anthony. On the court we're all about business, but the rest of the time we find many ways to have fun. The restaurant owner took one of the live lobsters out of the tank to show a few of the players. Charde asked if she could hold the lobster in order to play a joke on CD. When Charde snuck up behind her with the lobster in hand, CD glanced to her right, to find it an inch away from her nose! She screamed and almost fell out of her chair as Charde dangled its claws over her head. We all got a good kick out of it; but now it's back to business and preparing for our first game.

SUNDAY, MARCH 23, 2008

One thing I love about playing for Connecticut is that I have a family away from home. We've spent many holidays together, often on the road.

Thankfully, our coaches find ways to make them all special. In celebration of Easter, CD organized a scavenger hunt. We were split into three different teams and given clues inside of plastic Easter eggs. Things get pretty ugly whenever we have contests or play games. We get a little too competitive because we all want to win, even if it's as silly as a game of Pictionary or a hand of cards. Today, of course, there were accusations of cheating, and more than a few fighting words were thrown back and forth. I'm sure you can guess who won. That's right, yours truly, along with Tahirah, Kaili, Cassie, and managers Justine and Vinny.

Not only was today Easter; but it was also Coach's birthday. Our program has a tradition for birthday celebrations. We always sing Happy Birthday; and then we continuously chant a song until the person skips a lap around the room. Coach loves being a smart aleck, so he refused to get out of his seat, which meant we had to keep singing the song over and over again. When he finally got up, we all thought he would skip, but he tricked us and walked over to grab some food from a nearby table. After a few minutes, he finally attempted to skip, but I'd classify it more as a prance. But really, who am I to judge the skipping ability of a 54-year-old man?

Tonight we played our first-round game against Cornell and won 89-47. Everyone had a great attitude going into the game, and it showed because we played with a lot of heart and energy. Our team has the mentality that we are the best team in the country; our task now is to prove it over five more games.

In the gym, there were large-screen televisions hanging on the walls directly across from our bench. The screens showed our game live on ESPN, so the players on the bench could see themselves when the camera was pointed their way. It was awkward because everyone had to pretend they weren't on TV and act completely normal. Well, everyone except Tina. When it panned the bench, she looked directly into the camera, and made a funny face with her tongue out. I guess she didn't realize the coaches could see the screen as well as she could. CD shot Tina that "CD look," which means you're doing something wrong.

Later, I was talking to Kalana on the bench when I noticed we were on the big screen. "We're on TV!" I exclaimed as I nudged Kalana, acting like I had never been on television before.

After the game, a friend from school called asking, "Did you say 'we're on TV' when it panned to you on the bench?"

"Ha! You saw that? Yea, I guess I did." It's probably not a good idea to have big-screen televisions directly in front of the players!

Even when we're on the road, we can't get away from rehab. On Friday, I was allowed to pivot for the first time. It was a little strange because I knew in the back of my mind that was how I tore my knee. There's an initial fear with each new exercise, but once I try it a few times, I realize I'm capable of doing it and those thoughts are erased. Each milestone I reach is exciting because it's a change of pace from the same, monotonous workout every day.

WEDNESDAY, MARCH 26, 2008

For practice sessions in the NCAA Tournament, each team is given only 60 minutes on the court. The officials are very strict about the time allotments. No player is allowed to touch the basketballs until the clock begins. On Tuesday, we were on the court a little early, so we had to find ways to amuse ourselves before our time started. Maya provided the entertainment by showing us her middle school cheerleading moves. If you think Maya's good at basketball, wait until you see this. She said she had to choose between her two talents in eighth grade because the seasons overlapped. I think she made the wrong decision. She had such a bright future in cheerleading.

During the tournament, Coach ends practice with a minute left on the clock so everyone can take a half-court shot at the buzzer. I don't know when this ritual started, but we've done it ever since I've been here. There are so many balls in the air at once that nobody can accurately follow the flight of their own ball. Usually everyone misses, but when one happens to go in, everybody fights, claiming it was their ball that went through the hoop. Charde always takes a victory lap around the court swearing she made it, regardless of whether any shots actually went in.

Last night we played Texas in our second round game. They are a pretty good team, but we took it to them from the opening tap. We dominated the entire game and won 89-55. It's perfect timing that my teammates are playing really well right now because March is when we have to be at our best.

Half-court shots after practice

Lorin didn't play in either of the games because her grades were *a little* lower than the standards we have for our team. She wasn't academically ineligible by the school, but Coach refused to let her play. There have been many times when Coach has held people out of games because he wasn't happy with their work ethic. He says, "I'd rather lose than play people like you." It's more important to Coach that we do things the right way than it is even to win. He didn't care that it was the NCAA Tournament. Lorin wasn't working hard enough in the classroom. He made her return to campus for her classes on Monday and Tuesday, while everyone else stayed in Bridgeport. We're all pretty upset with her because she let us down. We need her in the tournament, so she better work her butt off in the classroom for the next couple of weeks.

SUNDAY, MARCH 30, 2008

Now we're in Greensboro for the Regionals, where we play our third and fourth round games. We have to win both to go to the Final Four. During our open practice today, Maya challenged Renee to a shooting contest. These two are probably the most competitive people on our team, so it was pretty entertaining to watch. They began behind the three-point line in the corner. Maya hit one, and then Renee matched it. They made about 10 in a row before Maya moved back behind the out-of-bounds line. Then Maya got a little cocky and decided to shoot from behind the row of media tables. She was almost in the bleachers. CD glanced over and saw what Maya was doing and gave her the scowl. Meanwhile, Renee crept off to the side, like she had no part in what was going on. I'm not sure who actually won, but they're lucky I wasn't out there.

On days when we play at noon, we don't have time for shootaround. Instead, we walk through the plays in the hotel before breakfast. Our managers line the floor with tape to represent the lane, and we use an orange as the ball.

Renee and Maya shooting behind press row

An outsider walking by the room might think we're crazy—a bunch of girls running around throwing an orange back and forth at 7:00 in the morning!

During the tournament, the NCAA gives a random drug test to four people on each team. I don't know if I look like I do drugs, but I get chosen every time there is a drug test. The whole process is strange because we have to go to the bathroom with someone standing right in front of us. Jacquie had to pee really badly, but couldn't do it once the observer started watching her. The rest of us were all laughing at her, which probably didn't help. Forty-five minutes later she finally made it back to the locker room.

Today, we played Old Dominion in the first round of the Regional Tournament. We won 78-63. The game was pretty physical and a couple of our players got banged up, but we survived. Rutgers fans were at our game with Old Dominion signs around their necks. I'm sure they'd rather play ODU than have to beat us to go to the Final Four.

MONDAY AFTERNOON, MARCH 31, 2008

Coach has a unique way of motivating his team. Sometimes he screams, other times he doesn't say a word, but he always knows how to get the best out of us. After practice today, he said, "There are three types of people in the world. There are wolves, who are bad people that only want for themselves. Next, there are sheep who don't get in anybody's way; they just go through life happy and peacefully. And then there are sheep dogs. Only a very small percentage of people are sheep dogs. They're the ones the sheep might not necessarily like, but when the wolf comes, they hide behind the sheep dogs because they know they'll be protected.

"Every team needs a couple sheep dogs. I know we have a couple of them on our team. If our opponents have one wolf, we need one sheep dog. But, what if a whole pack of wolves comes at us? Will we have enough sheep dogs to fight back? That's what this tournament comes down to. Do we have enough people who are going to step up and take control when the sh*t hits the fan? That's what we have to find out in the next couple days."

I believe in my teammates, and I think we're ready.

MONDAY NIGHT, MARCH 31, 2008

We have a roommate rotation of three different people on the road. This year, my roommates are Lorin, Tina, and Jaquie. Tina and I were staying together for the few days in Greensboro. She hasn't been playing well during this tournament. She doesn't look confident, and she isn't carrying herself the way she usually does. I don't know what's wrong with her. I tried to talk to her the night before the Old Dominion game. I asked her if anything was wrong, but she told me she was fine. I said, "Just be confident in yourself. You don't look like yourself out there, and we need you. This is my last chance and I no longer have any control over it. You won't know what it feels like until you're a senior, but at least try to understand where I'm coming from. Every game in the tournament could be the last time you ever step out on the floor. Keep your head up and get that swagger back and you'll be fine."

Tina talked with me for a while, and I could tell she cared deeply about what I was saying. She was doing her best to understand, but I don't know if it's really possible for a sophomore to get it. Not until she's a senior will she fully comprehend how we feel right now.

I became emotional during our conversation because I felt helpless. I couldn't contribute anything on the floor, and I didn't think my words were having an effect either. Tina came out the next day and looked exactly the same. I watched her practice, and I was really nervous about what I saw. I didn't think she was ready. I knew she would be a huge key for us to beat Rutgers and continue our season. I had already talked to her, and that didn't seem to work, so I didn't know what else to do.

Finally I had an idea that I thought might work. Tina seeks Coach's approval so desperately that I think it hurts her sometimes. Every time she messes up, she always looks over at the bench. I've watched from the sidelines much of the year, so I have listened to Coach's commentary all the time. He would say, "What on earth is Tina looking at?" or "What the hell am I gonna do for her over here?" It drove me crazy. Whenever Tina was playing well, she was completely in the game. It was when she was playing poorly that she would glance over—like Coach was going to give her some magical look that would help her make a layup. I thought Coach might be the one person who could help her.

We watched the film of Rutgers last night in a conference room downstairs in the hotel. After the film was over, I hung back to talk to Coach. He came up to me and said, "How are you doing with all this?"

"I'm fine," I responded.

He knew something was up, so he asked again, "What's wrong with you?"

"I'm really worried about Tina," I replied. I told him everything—about the conversation I had with her, and that I didn't know if it did any good. I said, "Honestly, I think you are the one person whose opinion she really cares about. If you think she sucks, she's gonna think she sucks. I know you're trying to teach her a lesson like you did to me, like you do to everyone that comes here, so they'll be stronger in the long run. But for me, I don't have a long run. I only have tomorrow. I don't have time to see if she's mature enough to handle it. I think she's a baby. She's not mentally tough enough. She's not at a point where she's going to find confidence from within. She's too messed up right now. I think you need to be on her side tomorrow. She needs your support more than anything."

He listened to my whole story, then said, "Bring everybody back down here."

I said, "What?" At this point it was almost *11:00*.

"Go get everyone and bring them back down here."

"Right now?"

"Yea. Go." So I ran up and caught a few people before they got to their rooms. We called everyone else and gave them the message. Everybody was confused, asking, "What's going on? What did we do?" I didn't really know what to tell them. I had no idea what Coach had planned. I knew this meeting was my doing, so I was a little nervous for what was about to happen.

We all sat down in the room, and everyone was looking at each other wondering what the hell was going on. Coach came in and started pacing around the room. "Something's wrong here. Something isn't right. We don't have everybody here as a part of what's going on. We're missing one key guy. One guy who we are all counting on—but we have no idea if she's gonna be there for us when we need her." Then he asked Renee who this person was. Everyone was aware that Tina wasn't doing what she was capable of. Renee guessed, "TT?" which is her nickname for Tina.

"Tina Charles. Tina Charles is the one guy we don't know if we can count on." Coach asked me, "What is the one word that comes to your mind when you think of Tina?"

I said, "Unsure, baby, immature."

Coach said, "Baby. How does that make you feel that your teammates think you're a baby?"

"Embarrassed," Tina replied.

Then I said, "I don't doubt that she can do it. I know she can. It's just a matter of getting it done."

Coach said, "Oh, we all know she can do it." Then he looked directly at Tina and continued, "No one here is challenging your athletic ability or judging you as a person. We're just wondering if you are mature enough to step up for all your teammates."

Then Coach talked about how much trust he had in some of our key guys. He said, "Keesh, if this was two or three years ago, I would have never for a second trusted you; but you've grown up and matured so much, especially this year. I know you're gonna do what you've done all year.

"Brit, when you were Tina's age, I thought you were one of the most immature basketball players I've ever coached. You've matured a lot with everything you've been through with your knee, and I really respect that. I know you will make a huge contribution in whatever minutes you can play.

"Charde, after everything you've been through, do I trust you with my life? Yea, I do. Not with my kids' lives, but, yea, I trust you with my life.

"Renee, Maya, I know what you guys are gonna do. We can't expect everything from a freshman, but I'm confident that you're going to go out there and do what you've been doing all year."

He asked us all, "I want you to raise your hands and tell me what you really think. Not what you think I want to hear. How many of you think we can't win without Tina?" About half of the team raised their hands. He said, "You know, that's good. You guys realize how much we need her in order to win tomorrow. But you know what I like even more? I like you cocky guys who think we're good enough to win without her."

"We're gonna do this tomorrow, and we're gonna do it with or without Tina." His eyes focused on Tina, "Tomorrow we're gonna see what you're made of, Tina Charles. Does anybody else want to say anything?"

It was quiet for a minute, then Brit said, "After this, I'm not playin' ball anymore. We've been through a lot, and I just want to validate what we've done. I don't want tomorrow to be my last game." Tears streaked down her face as she spoke.

I followed up by saying, "When you're young, you think you have all the time in the world. But we don't. I never in a million years thought the game last year against LSU would be my last chance to play in the NCAA Tournament. You only have 40 minutes guaranteed, so make the best of it. I wish I could be out there with you guys more than anything in the world. I believe in you guys. I'm so proud of you, and I know you can do it."

Then Coach said with a laugh, "Listen to these guys. They sound like some selfish sons of b*tches, don't they?"

"So what? We have a right to be," I replied.

"Damn right, you do. You seniors have been here for four years and experienced more than any of these other guys. This is your last chance, and they won't understand that until they're your age. So you seniors have a right to be selfish now. All of my best players have been a little selfish. They've wanted something so bad that they put their personal desires first, and in reaching those, the rest of the team got to experience them too."

Coach was exactly right. The younger guys have no idea how we're feeling, and I don't expect them to. When I was their age, I didn't understand. Now, it's scary to think my career can end at any moment. All I know is that tomorrow is not going to be that moment.

When I approached Coach last night, I wasn't trying to tell him how to coach. He's won five National Championships. I just wanted to help Tina. I've been in her position, and I know how it feels. All athletes have times in their careers when they are a little unsure of themselves, and they need some extra support. That's the best part about playing on a team. We all have our teammates to pick us up when we're down, and also to kick us in the butt when we need it.

I left the room feeling better. I hope what we said got through to her. I don't know if it helped, but I don't want to look back and wish I had done something more. I don't want to have any regrets. This is what it all comes down to, and I embraced my role on the team. If support is all I can give my teammates, then I'll give as much as I can. After I called Tina an unsure, immature baby, we had to walk back to our room together. She knows I love her, and I only want the best for her. I think she understands that, which is why she wasn't upset. She's a good kid, who loves basketball and her teammates. If I didn't think she could do it, I wouldn't have wasted my time. I believe in her and know she'll play great tomorrow.

TUESDAY, APRIL 1, 2008

We just beat Rutgers 66-56 and we're going to the Final Four! I am so excited that I don't even know what to say. Tina played great. She had nine points, 12 rebounds, and four blocks. I'm really proud of her. I'm going to celebrate with my teammates now.

WEDNESDAY, APRIL 2, 2008

It's hard to find words to explain how I felt last night. No one on our team has ever been to the Final Four, so it's a huge accomplishment for all of us. We couldn't have played much worse in the first half, trailing by as many as 14. We were still down by five at halftime, but everyone stayed poised, calm, and confident that it was still our game to win.

In the second half, I felt it was only a matter of time before we took the lead; but time was running out. Watching the game from the bench, I looked up at the clock. 12 minutes. 10 minutes. And we were still behind. The minutes went by like seconds. So many thoughts were running through my head. I tried to stay positive, but the scoreboard wasn't helping. I tried to avoid it, but the question kept popping into my head, "What if this is my last game?"

"No, this can't be my last game. We're gonna pull this out."

In my head, I was carrying on a full conversation with myself—like a crazy person. I was a rollercoaster of emotions. Nothing was going our way. But then, with six minutes to go, I glanced at Renee and saw the look in her eyes. They were full of fire and determination, and I knew there was no way we

Renee—determined to win

would lose. Renee's confidence and will to win became contagious, and all of a sudden, we were in command.

With 17 seconds left on the clock, I lost it. Coach looked down the bench at me and I was sobbing, like the crybaby I am. He walked over and gave me a big bear hug and said, "I knew this would happen for you. You were a huge part in getting us here." A few seconds later, the buzzer rang, and the celebration began. I'm not cleared to run yet, but sprinting onto the court to embrace my teammates seemed like a good idea at the time. Kai wrapped her arms around me and gave me a huge hug. She said, "This is for you."

Emotional hug from Coach

Bringing down the net after the Regional Final

After we received the trophy, it was time to cut down the nets. I don't know whose bright idea it was to tell Lorin to go first because she never has any idea what's going on. She didn't understand what she was supposed to do, so we had to explain to her, in a step-by-step process, how to cut a piece of string. When it was Kaili's turn to go, she said, "Somebody better hold this ladder down." Everyone started laughing as Renee and Charde ran to her rescue. My teammates nominated me to be the last one to climb on the ladder, which was an amazing feeling. They knew how much this meant to me, and they wanted to fulfill my dream. My face was stained with tears, but I didn't care because it felt so good to bring the net down.

Reporters have asked me all year, "How would you feel if your class was the first senior class since 1990 to never reach the Final Four?"

Photo courtesy of Cloe Poisson / *Hartford Courant*   Photo courtesy of UConn Athletic Communications

"We're planning on going, so there's no reason to think about what would happen if we don't," I would respond.

"But what if it didn't happen?" they'd probe further.

"I'm confident it will. You'll have to ask me in March because I already told you what I know will happen." Now, there are no more "what ifs?" We made it, and there's nothing more they can say!

Nothing in my life has ever felt so rewarding. It's for moments like this that we play the game. We set our sights on something really hard to do, and accomplishing it together is a remarkable feeling. We've overcome some very difficult challenges this year, and we really deserve to go to the Final Four. It's a dream come true, but I'm still dreaming of more.

THURSDAY, APRIL 3, 2008

We arrived in Tampa today for the Final Four. When we entered the hotel, we were greeted by people dressed in pirate costumes, who placed beads around our necks. The hotel was elaborately decorated with Final Four and UConn signs, and there were giant pictures of our team everywhere. A huge sandcastle with the Final Four logo had been built in the middle of the lobby. The hotel staff immediately took us to a reception with refreshments of fresh fruit, fondue, and other hors d'oeuvres. We also received Lebron James bags stuffed with Final Four apparel, watches, sunglasses and shoes. It was great to be welcomed in such an extravagant manner.

FRIDAY, APRIL 4, 2008

This morning, we went to the presentation of the Women's Basketball Coaches' Association All-America Team. Renee and Maya were both chosen as top-10 players in the country. It was really exciting to see them receive the recognition they deserve. After that we had an autograph session outside the Forum. I was amazed at the number of Connecticut fans who were there, waiting in line in the sweltering heat. The atmosphere here is electric, and we can't wait to play

During practice this afternoon, Kalana and I did rehab as usual. Today was the first time I was allowed to jump. Gyms on the road seldom have the same equipment we use in our training room at home, so we have to be creative with our workouts. We improvised by jumping off coolers and stepping up onto bleachers. I only have a couple more weeks until I'm allowed to start jogging, and I'm so excited. I never thought I would look forward to running.

Tonight, we went to the Final Four Salute reception at the Tampa Convention Center for all the teams participating. We were again greeted by the pirates, and then a beautiful yacht took us to the ceremony. It had three levels, with a dining room, a dance floor, and a bar. It was a little awkward at first because the players were expected to mingle with their opponents. After a while, it turned more cordial, and the players started making their way out to the dance floor. A few minutes later, a dance-off began between our team and LSU. All four teams were soon crowded around the dance floor, cheering on the competition. A player from LSU would dance in the middle of the circle, and then one of our players would match it. This battle went back and forth for a few minutes until Charde completely stole the spotlight and no one else could compete.

All dressed up for the Final Four Salute Winner

SUNDAY, APRIL 6, 2008

Tonight we played Stanford for the opportunity to advance to the National Championship game. Before the game, Coach told us, "There are a million kids around the country wishing they could be in your shoes right now. You have one chance that you've been waiting for your whole life, and this is it. We've worked all year for this, and we're ready." I had goose bumps up and down my arms as he finished. I wished I could be out there more than ever, but I was still happy to be a part of it.

From the opening tip, it didn't look good. We were behind the entire game, and I kept waiting for us to make our run. We finally did. We cut Stanford's lead to one with 14 minutes left; but they had an answer. Every time Stanford needed to make a big play, or make a big shot—they did. They just played better than us tonight. After everything we prepared for all year, it came down to one game. One night. It didn't matter that we were the better team all year because tonight, for 40 minutes, they proved they deserved to win. I can't believe it's over.

After the game, I started crying before we even got off the court. I couldn't believe this was my last game as a UConn basketball player. By the time we made it to the locker room, I was sobbing. I sat down, and I couldn't say anything. I didn't know what to say. All I could do was cry. I cried harder than I think I have ever cried in my life. When Coach came in to speak with us, I was actually shaking. Tears were running down my hands onto the floor, and I didn't care. I can't even tell you what Coach said. I couldn't function. I couldn't talk. I was just taking up space. As soon as he finished, I went right to the bathroom and locked myself in a stall. CD kept knocking on the door, trying to get me to open it. I finally did, and she gave me a comforting hug and tried to calm me down. I was literally hyperventilating. I was trying to talk back, but I couldn't. Every word was interrupted with a hiccup or a breath. "You gave it everything you had, and you have nothing to be ashamed about," she said. When she finally got me to start breathing normally, she told me I had to return to the locker room because the media was coming in.

When I got back, I curled up inside one of the lockers. The camera people flocked to me, probably thinking, "Look, she's crying the hardest. Let's go take

Leaving a piece of me behind, forever

her picture!" With my hair matted to my face and my eyes red and puffy, I looked like death. I really wanted to kick them all in their faces. They were sticking their cameras 12 inches from my face while I was having a nervous breakdown. After they left, I went around and gave every person on my team a hug and told them I loved them. It was extremely emotional. Everyone on the team was crying, but I was by far the worst. Kaili told me she was sorry they couldn't do it for me, and Maya said the same. The underclassmen felt like they had let down the seniors. They have another shot, but we don't. I felt the exact same way when Barbara, Ann, Will, and Nicole graduated. I told Maya, "You've got three more years. You better come out with three of 'em. I'll be expecting it." She promised me she would. And she's good enough to make it happen.

After everyone left the locker room to go and see their families, I couldn't move. I was paralyzed. I just sat in that locker. I tried to make it last as long as I could. For some reason, I felt that when I left the locker room that night, a piece of me would be gone forever. I tried to hang on as long as I could, so I just sat there alone. I sat there and cried until I couldn't cry anymore.

I can honestly say that I gave everything I had to UConn Basketball. The more a person puts into something, the more it hurts to lose it. I felt like something was dropped on my chest and hurt my heart. While I was playing, I treated every drill like it was the most important thing in the world. I killed myself every time we had conditioning, with every sprint I ran. I gave it my best, but my best wasn't good enough.

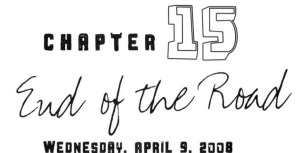

CHAPTER 15
End of the Road

WEDNESDAY, APRIL 9, 2008

We flew home the morning following the game. It sucks to be back on campus, knowing we should still be in Tampa. I don't want to go out in public. I don't want to go to class. I don't want to do anything but mope. The National Championship was last night. I couldn't watch a second of it. I didn't even care to know the score.

Today, my teammates gathered together in the training room to watch the WNBA draft, while Kalana and I did our rehab. Ketia was in the office with Coach, and Charde stayed behind in Tampa because she had been invited to the draft. I expected Ketia to go in the second round, but when they called her name at number 12, we jumped up and sprinted down to Coach's office. We bombarded her as she smiled from ear to ear. I am very proud of her because she has come such a long way. If anyone told us four years ago that Ketia would be drafted in the first round, we would have said they were crazy. It's a tribute to her hard work, and she deserves it all. We continued to watch the draft in Coach's office until Charde finally got picked in the third round—pick number 30.

THURSDAY, APRIL 17, 2008

Whenever one of my eyelashes falls out, I follow the same ritual. I place it on the end of my finger and blow it off as I make a wish. For as long as I can remember, my wish has been to win a National Championship. Today, as my eyelash blew away, "I want to win a National Championship" instinctively popped into my head. It was a little sad; but I laughed at how it was programmed into my brain. I finally feel okay letting it go.

I'm still a dreamer, so I'm sure there will be many more to come. I hope I'll find something new in my life to love as much as I've loved playing at UConn.

MONDAY, APRIL 21, 2008

Our apartment is so lonely. Ketia and Charde left campus within a week of being drafted, so now it's just Brit and me. It was really strange to watch them clean out their rooms. It seemed they were packing up their lives and leaving only an empty space behind.

Their rooms are quiet now, waiting for new students to move in and bring them back to life, and fill their walls with memories. I hope they'll be painted with as many laughs and good times as were ours.

The thought of leaving UConn is heartbreaking. I never imagined this day would actually come. Everything these past few weeks has been bittersweet.

THURSDAY, MAY 8, 2008

The past week, I've spent each night in Gampel finishing my final projects and studying for exams. I've spent countless hours in this building—hanging out between classes, napping in the locker room, waiting for practice, studying, writing papers, meeting with tutors. Sometimes I've been here from noon to midnight. Not because I had to, but because it was my home.

I took my last exam today. I thought I'd be ecstatic to be finished with school, but that wasn't the case. As much as I hated studying for all those years, I didn't want it to be over. I was the last one in my exam room because I knew that walking out the door meant college was over.

SUNDAY, MAY 11, 2008

When I woke up this morning, I felt strange knowing that in just a few hours I would be a college graduate. Then I received my diploma, and it was all over. This chapter of my life has ended; and a new one has begun. I have no idea where this new chapter will take me or what challenges it will present.

For four years, everything in my life has made sense. I have known what I was doing every day, and I was always focused on a goal. Now, I am forced to make decisions that will determine my future. I want to continue playing basketball for a few years. I hope to go overseas in the fall, as soon as I'm cleared to play, but many questions remain.

The one thing I know for sure is that I'll always have a home in Connecticut. When we graduated, Coach told us that his house, the locker room, and the gym would be open to us for the rest of our lives. This program has a lifelong fan in me.

When I look back on all the great memories I've had at Connecticut, I won't remember the scores of every game. All the awards, the trophies, the rings, the watches—they're all nice; but 20 years down the road, when I think of Connecticut Basketball, I'm going to think of my teammates and the times we shared. We laughed together, we cried together, and we grew up together. It's comforting to know we'll have a connection to each other for the rest of our lives.

Graduation day with Coach

I came to Connecticut thinking it was to play basketball. Four years later, I understand it was to learn about life. I'll never be able to thank Coach enough for all he has done for me. He's had a huge impact on my character and values. He wants to make us better people even more than he wants to make us the best basketball players. Coach has motivated us to play for our teammates and to be a part of something bigger than ourselves. He taught me many lessons that I will carry with me in everything I do. I can only hope to find another situation in my life where I'll be surrounded by people with so much passion.

Basketball has taken me on an unbelievable journey—far beyond what I ever expected. I've met so many different people. I've seen the country. I've seen the world. All the sacrifices, all the sweat, all the blood, all the tears—it was all worth it. Every second of it.

Looking back on my career, I realize that basketball has been much more to me that just a sport. Basketball has changed my life and shaped me into the person I am today. It has taught me I can accomplish anything I put my mind to.

I know I have given everything I had, so when I look in the mirror, I'm extremely proud of the person I see.

Nothing has been handed to me. Everything I have accomplished has been the result of years and years of hard work. My passion and love for the game have taken me everywhere I wanted to go.

I have never been the most athletic or talented player. I am just an ordinary person with an extraordinary heart—the heart of a Husky.

Appreciations

First of all, I would like to thank my mom, dad, and brother for being so supportive of every crazy idea I've had in my life. I appreciate their help with this project.

Thanks to all my teammates over all the years for being my best friends and making basketball so much fun. Thanks to all my coaches who have contributed to my development not only as a basketball player, but also as a person. I deeply appreciate the impact they have had on my life.

A special thanks to my editor and friend, Warren Witherell, for coming into my life. He was truly a gift from God at a time when I was searching for someone to guide me through this process. *Heart of a Husky* would not have been possible without his help. He was instrumental in turning my dream into a reality. Not many people would put their lives on hold for two months to help a complete stranger. Through hundreds of phone calls, emails, and a visit to Cincinnati, we have grown from strangers to good friends. I've learned more from him than I ever imagined was possible. Warren has touched a multitude of people throughout his life, and he has truly been an inspiration to me. I can never thank him enough.

I would like to thank the following people from Keen Communications— President Richard Hunt, Editorial Director Jack Heffron, and Media and Marketing Director Howard Cohen. They were willing to take a chance on me, especially after I told them two days after our first meeting that I'd be moving to Ireland. They have been extremely accommodating and understanding of the situation. It has been a true pleasure to work with them.

Thanks to my book designer, Steve Sullivan, for his brilliant artistic ability. As you can see from the book in your hands, he is very good at his job. It has been great fun to work with him.

Thanks to Paula Schute for reading and re-reading my book more times than she would like to remember. I'm not sure how she got dragged into being an editor, a graphic designer, a web designer, and a publicist, but I truly appreciate everything she's done. God love ya, Ms. Schute!

Thanks to Ellen Boyne for her careful and professional editing.

I appreciate the hard work of Randy Press and the UConn Athletic Department for providing many of the photographs that enrich this book.

Thanks to the *Hartford Courant* and the *Republican-American* for providing additional photographs.

Thanks to the many people who have read drafts and offered their suggestions. Their insight has been valuable throughout the development of this book.

Thanks to my all fans and loved ones for reading this book. I appreciate all their support throughout my career.